ZERO TOLERANCE OR COMMUNITY TOLERANCE?

*This book is dedicated to Paul Ormerod,
1961-1998, and all his friends.*

Zero Tolerance or Community Tolerance?

Managing crime in high crime areas

SANDRA WALKLATE
Manchester Metropolitan University

KAREN EVANS
Manchester City Council

ASHGATE

Published by
Ashgate Publishing Limited
Gower House
Croft Road
Aldershot
Hants
GU11 3HR
England

Ashgate Publishing Company
Suite 420
101 Cherry Street
Burlington, VT 05401-4405
USA

Ashgate website: http://www.ashgate.com

British Library Cataloguing in Publication Data
Walklate, Sandra
  Zero tolerance or community tolerance? : managing crime in
  high crime areas
  1. Crime prevention - Citizen participation 2. Crime -
  Sociological aspects 3. Crime - Regional disparities
  I. Title II. Evans, Karen, 1961 -
  364.4'045'61

Library of Congress Control Number: 99-72973

Reprinted 2003

ISBN 0 7546 1017 9

Printed in Great Britain by Biddles Limited,
Guildford and King's Lynn.

Contents

List of Figures

List of Tables

Preface and Acknowledgements

The work presented in this book was supported under the ESRC's Law and Social Order Initiative grant no. L21025036 and was conducted between February 1994 to August 1996. During that time the project was supported in a range of different ways by people too numerous to mention. However particular credit should be given to Penny Fraser who started as part of the project team and subsequently secured a post with NACRO and Linda Harvey who ended as part of the project team. Each of these people, in quite different ways, left their mark on the work produced here. Professor Tim Hope, as the director of this initiative also leant his support at crucial moments. In addition it is important to mention particular people who eased the research process for us especially Nigel Bonson and Ann Weir of Safer Salford, Councillor Jim King, the (then) Chief Superintendent Colin Cramphorn and (then) Superintendent Roger Roberts. Indeed Safer Salford, Salford City Council, and the police officers of 'F' Division of Greater Manchester Police could not have been more helpful or accommodating throughout the course of the research. We hope we have repaid their help with the arguments presented here.

Particular mention should be made of our interviewing team who worked diligently, professionally and reliably; Linda Burch, Gary Kelly, Tony Kearon, Gaynor Bagnall, Jane Franklin, Elaine Lusty, Caroline Clayton, Lynne Greenwood, Elliot Costello, Brian Macdonald and Prue Yeoman.

Of course, we are also grateful for the support and participation of all the residents, community groups, local agencies and businesses who took part in the research. Without their willing help and assistance this work would not have been possible. Despite living in areas 'over-researched' such willingness to help should not be taken for granted. Unfortunately we cannot name all the people who participated and helped in this way as we undertook to maintain both confidentiality and anonymity.

An especial thanks is due to Sheila Walker, who prepared the camera ready copy for this book. Last but by no means least Karen would like to acknowledge the support of Colin Morrison and Sandra, that of Ron Wardale who actually thought of the title of this book and much more besides.

Parts of this text have appeared elsewhere as journal articles and we would like to acknowledge the following for copyright permission to reproduce some of that material here; *Sociological Review*, vol. 44. no. 3. August 1996 Evans, Fraser and Walklate; Whom can you trust? The politics of 'grassing' on an inner city housing estate. *The British Journal of Sociology*, vol. 49, no. 4 December 1998 Walklate; Crime and community; fear or trust? *Theoretical Criminology* (Sage Publications) vol. 2 no. 4 November 1998 Walklate; Excavating the fear of crime: fear, anxiety or trust? *Crime Prevention and Community Safety: An International Journal* (1999) Evans and Walklate; Zero tolerance or community tolerance: police and community talk about crime in high crime areas, vol.1 no. 1 and Walklate; Some questions about community safety partnerships, vol. 1, no. 3; published by Perpetuity Press Limited, P.O. Box 376, Leicester, LE2 3ZZ. And finally, Evans (1997) It's alright round here if you're local: community in the inner city. In P. Hoggett (ed) *Contested Communities. Experiences, Struggles, Policies.* Bristol: Policy Press.

Karen Evans
Sandra Walklate
Manchester, February 1999

Part One: Crime and Community

Introduction: Ways of Thinking About Community

Preamble

In 1997 the new Labour government made clear its commitment to ensuring that crime prevention would become a statutory duty of local government (indeed this commitment had been pledged by the then Opposition spokesman on crime - Jack Straw, at a conference, 'Crime - the Local Solution', organised by the Local Government (LGA) Association in March 1997). In the light of this commitment local authority personnel up and down Britain were charged with the writing of corporate community safety strategies. At the same time the 1996 Internationl Criminal Victimisation Survey suggested that these personnel will be working in a context of comparatively high national rates of crime which the British Crime Survey of 1996 estimated had risen 91% since 1985. This fast growing rate of crime has initiated much discussion in the public domain around law and order issues. Much of this discussion has revolved around the impact of such a high crime rate, and associated significant fear of crime, on the quality of life of people living in England and Wales. There has also been a great deal of debate on differing ways to manage the crime problem (Garland, 1996) with the significant emergence of the concept of community safety in the mid 1980s driven by the idea that the solution to an area's crime problems lay in co-operation between community and law-enforcement agencies. The 1990s, however, has seen the debate around the concept of Zero Tolerance policing exported from America to Britain, which arguably signals a move away from the emphasis on community solutions to crime problems. Although ostensibly closely linked to the idea of community safety, zero tolerance in fact substitutes the notion of a complete respite from crime and incivilities for the community, where no infringement of criminal or civil statutes is tolerated. The zero tolerance policing style is justified by

3

Good Ref

reference to community wants and needs but, due to its blanket coverage, it cannot recognise different degrees of tolerance which exist within a community, or between one community and another. Zero Tolerance policing posits a crime-free environment as the goal of every 'law-abiding' individual, without offering any degree of subtlety or attempting to understand the many dynamics of community relationships which are in existence or the diversity of responses to crime demonstrated by individuals.

Introduction

The arguments put forward in this book look to introduce such a subtlety to the understanding of the management of crime in high crime communities and derive from a longitudinal research study which took place over a two and a half year period. From 1994 to 1996 researchers based at the University of Salford and the University of Keele embarked on research into two similarly structured neighbourhoods within the city of Salford in the North of England. This research set out to situate an understanding of the risk from and fear of crime in a comparative, urban context - to uncover how people who live, work and go to school in designated 'high-crime' areas manage their routine daily lives and construct their own responses to 'risk of' and 'fear of' crime. We were interested to document the personal and individual ways in which the research subjects managed their own fear of crime and to what extent these management practices were informed by their own perceptions as to which actions were risky and which were safe within a local context.

The two areas chosen for the study were inner-city wards (to anonymise these places they have been named Oldtown and Bankhill), similarly structured in socio-economic terms, though physically different. Both wards were perceived to be areas of high deprivation, sharing many characteristics and indicators of poverty with many other areas of British cities which might be said to be 'in crisis'. They were therefore locations in which those who utilise the term might assume an 'underclass' would be found and we will refer to this assumption later in the text, questioning both the assumption and the application of the term to any of the research subjects located in these areas. Although the empirical data presented in the following chapters relates to these two North of England wards, we argue that the similarity which they display to other wards across Britain, means that the findings generated have a clear resonance above and beyond the particular locations featured. The findings which will be presented address issues which are of concern to criminology, sociology, social policy and politics. The findings will contribute to an understanding of community, social exclusion, crime prevention policies and the meaning of social dis/organisation. They address too some fundamental questions regarding the salience of the fear of crime debate and the contribution which an understanding of community tolerance can make to this important debate and other national and local crime management policies.

Talk about community in criminology

The history of the study of community is one which is well rehearsed - from the rejection of the study of community in the 1960s to its replacement with the study of 'locality' during the 1980s. These locality studies recognised that:

> People's location within particular places tended to be an important aspect of their lived experience.... and is a major resource drawn upon for many purposes (Day and Murdoch 1993:84)

Some such studies also argued that a 'locality effect' existed, which meant policy-makers and practitioners adopting different policies in different areas in order to remain sensitive to the effects of local culture and political and social systems (Brownill, 1993; Day and Murdoch, 1993; Savage et al, 1987). However, the study of community itself was seen as outdated - with little to offer the contemporary context.

Within criminology, however, the theme of community has remained a recurrent one. Community has been investigated as a way of understanding the existence of criminal activity, explaining crime patterns and, as a result, the appeal to community, has also played a major part in crime prevention policies (Hope, 1995). Hope argues that these interventions have been informed by differing paradigms which are in turn informed by different ideas of community. Hope charts community-based crime prevention practices, from the Chicago School's Chicago Area Project, established in the 1930s (the disorganised community), through the input of community work up to the 1970s (the disadvantaged community) and the appeal to the community's surveillance of itself (the frightened community), which became fashionable in the 1970s in the US and the 1980s in the UK (through ideas like Neighbourhood Watch).

Despite the different political complexions of these crime prevention paradigms, Hope argues, all these approaches have in common the belief that:

> ...community structure itself shapes local rates of crime - that community crime rates may be the result of something more than the mere aggregation of individual propensities for criminality or victimisation. (Hope, 1995:129)

and, as a consequence, those active in the field of community crime prevention have looked to alter, strengthen or enlist existing community organisations and the activities of community members in order to reduce crime in residential neighbourhoods. The setting up community-based projects for the unemployed and for youth, Neighbourhood Watch schemes, encouraging self-help groups and tenants associations, moving council offices out of the Town Halls and into neighbourhoods, have all been advocated at one time or another as methods of empowering communities or involving communities in improving their particular conditions.

However, these appeals to community have been inadequately explored, theorised or evaluated. Current research understanding tells us that the mobilisation of community around any issues, but certainly in crime prevention practices, has most appeal in the more wealthy areas of predominantly owner-occupied housing which have stable populations and residents with the time and skills to divert to such activity; and that they are less successful in low-income, heterogeneous neighbourhoods with more transient population bases and where crime is high (Hope and Shaw, 1988). These are areas where, according to Skogan, residents are:

> deeply suspicious of one another, report only a weak sense of community, have low levels of influence on neighbourhood events...and feel that it is their neighbours whom they must watch carefully. (Skogan, 88:45)

Our work in Salford suggests that this is an oversimplification and that poorer, inner-city neighbourhoods far from being the disorganised neighbourhoods of popular representation, may exhibit many and different community structures and patterns of local organisation and networks.

In order to understand fully the play of forces which shape local communities, their responses to local conditions and what prevents or allows effective community organisation itself, there needs to be a greater emphasis on these communities themselves in order to understand more fully, and more adequately, the conditions under which community crime prevention or community safety strategies might be successful or might fail either in their own terms or in others' terms. We will argue that a significant reason for the failure or limited success of such schemes or strategies is that they have failed to understand the specific dynamics operating in the communities in which they have been applied.

Managing communities

Received wisdom reports that lack of social control within inner city areas is likely to arise as a result of weak communities, a lack of social networks and a lack of concern about an area: where neighbourhood exists as a collection of disparate persons living in close proximity but not caring for community values. Thus, interventions into such areas aim to resurrect ideas of community, for example, local people are exhorted to watch out for one another, care for neighbours, work collectively for change and to liaise with and accept the input of professionals, whether police or local authorities. However, our work challenges the assumption that lack of community feeling or weak social bonds are the key determinants of social disorder within these areas.

Within both Oldtown and Bankhill, we argue community works on a number of different levels. Many local people whom we spoke to were closely linked to their local areas and recognised the importance of sustaining such links in order to maintain their own 'ontological security' (Giddens, 1991). In Bankhill we found community activists struggling to maintain community cohesion against incredible odds. In Oldtown community looked very different; the close ties which existed in the area meant that an organised criminal gang could claim to control the area and to sustain levels of intimidation and fear. As one local community activist from this ward told us:

> Everyone knows who this group is and what they are into at any particular time. This creates the fear - nothing is kept secret really and the grapevine is very active. The gang's exploits are known throughout the estate very quickly after any incident has occurred. People then

become wary of walking past this gang - they may be challenged as - because everyone knows what is happening - then everyone is a potential grass.

Rather than a lack of surveillance in this ward there is maintained a surveillance of local people by those involved in the criminal network, mainly young men, who maintain a vigilant gaze over the central part of the estate. It is a matter of importance and in need of some reflection, too, that despite the problems faced by local residents within both these wards, they opened their doors to our team of researchers and discussed, on their doorsteps and in their homes, issues of significance to their own lives which touched on extremely sensitive aspects of local social relations. Our experience strongly suggests that these areas are not the frightened maelstroms of some media, government and academic opinion but are areas where residents must find ways of coping with day-to-day issues of community, neighbourhood and locality and that they will work with others in an effort to find solutions.

Looking at the experience of crime in these two wards helps to reveal how people use their sense of community and of neighbourhood and how this can differ from place to place. Within the two wards in which we conducted our research very different strategies emerged. In Oldtown, we argue, your place in relation to crime places you in a community of belonging and exclusion; in Bankhill there is an absence even of this ordering. In Oldtown there exists a strong competing definition to a professional definition and application of community; in Bankhill there is an absence of trust beyond that shared by a few residents within very small areas or within social networks which have been built up over many years. Where trust is so limited that which is found can work to exclude individuals who are not party to a social scene or do not conform to certain roles and expectations. Given these differences and difficulties the question must be asked; what does community safety, community crime prevention or indeed community anything actually mean? Yet policy makers and practitioners still invoke the notion of 'community' without reference to how its different dimensions are actually experienced, intersect with one another and play a part in shaping local people's beliefs and behaviour.

A study of community?

The research methodology utilised for this project employed various data collection techniques including ethnographic fieldwork as well as a more traditional crime audit conducted through a survey of residential households and business and community organisations in both areas. We also conducted a series of focus group discussions with local people, school students and police officers employed in the local areas. Although crime statistics for the two areas were collected, it was only in the last six months of the research that a detailed analysis of recorded crime and incident data in both wards was attempted. In this respect then, it was not a piece of work which focused on crime itself, more the experience of crime. The methodology adopted, although including a crime audit, was not typical of the approach taken up since by many local authorities in their own crime audits - instead it placed primary importance on the lay perceptions of both the area and its community make-up. The methodology and viewpoint adopted allowed some very interesting findings to emerge. The two research sites, although seemingly so similar when official indicators were chosen to measure their position within the city, and geographically so close (they were less than two miles apart) actually exhibited very different responses to their situation. In the light of these findings it became clear that we were researching two very different areas, suggesting that crime prevention and community safety initiatives must be sensitive to these differences, involving the communities at very different levels and utilising quite clearly dissimilar techniques of intervention.

The starting point for our research was neighbourhood, voluntary organisation and community. The study of these wards did include an analysis of the place which crime played in these localities but other aspects of living in the localities were allowed to form an equally important dimension to the research. By focusing on a comparative study of two similarly structured areas of the one city we hoped to draw out the different ways in which residents and users of these places might respond and adapt to their local situation. We hoped to uncover different sets of relationships to and perceptions of crime which rooted in such variables as gender, occupation, age and class and use the concept of 'layering of community' (Massey,1995) to build upon the existing tradition within both sociology and criminology of examining the significance of the notion of community to an understanding of experiences of crime.

Increasingly the research began to focus on the dynamics of what might be called 'community' within the two wards. Crow and Allen (1994) define a study of community as disclosing:

> ... ways in which individuals are embedded into sets of personal relationships which are based outside the household. (Crow and Allen,1994:177)

We were interested in this notion of embeddedness, but through the course of the research were alerted to the idea that other relationships, apart from 'sets of personal relationships', come to play an important part in the way in which individuals feel within their localities, in how they behave and in how these sentiments and behaviours are expressed in the wider social context.

In this sense then, we became involved in a study of community and how this term 'community' resonated at a number of different levels within these inner-city neighbourhoods. We were conscious of the need to critically evaluate the term, not least because it is used with such regularity by those who are involved in the management and control of these areas and the people who live within them, but also because this term is so often uncritically invoked by both national and local government personnel who are concerned to 'make a difference' at a local level, in their quest to reduce fear, to lessen crime and its impact, and to increase the quality of life.

How people really talk about community

We were interested in whether the term 'community' did have any resonance for the local residents of Oldtown and Bankhill, whether it featured in the everyday understanding that they had of their neighbourhood or of the relationships that they had built up with others living nearby. We were unsure whether we would indeed find evidence of community solidarity in these areas in particular, where extreme disadvantage and deprivation are also found and whether notions of 'community', so prevalent in fictional and documentary accounts of the city of Salford in the early and mid twentieth century, could survive under the conditions of extreme instability and anxiety about the future and the present which are so much a feature of the late twentieth century. We were unsure, too, what forms 'community' might take under these conditions. So, what use did local people have for the term community?

During the survey we conducted of roughly three hundred local people in each ward, we asked respondents whether their area had a 'community feel'. Around 16% (46 out of 294 respondents in Oldtown) said 'yes it did' while approximately 11% (34 out of 302 respondents in Bankhill) agreed that their area had a community feel. Similar numbers respectively in each ward responded positively to the statement that the 'best thing about living here is the community'. However, this only tells us about the response to our suggestion that community may or may not exist and very little about what is actually meant by an affirmative or a negative response to this suggestion.

We recorded, on the questionnaire, any comments respondents made about 'community' during the course of the interview. The following are a sample of those comments:

> It's [referring to the area of residence] beginning to get a community feel. (Oldtown)
> [There are] no community spirits, some people are friendly, people move in and out very quickly. (Bankhill)
> Everybody knows me but it's not a community thing. (Bankhill)

These quotes revealed a number of things about how 'community' was perceived; perhaps most of all they revealed a lack of consensus as to what constituted a 'community'. Some respondents related the term to personal relationships built up in a particular and bounded physical area close to their own home, for others 'community' was more closely related to wider networks of support and to 'who you know' across the wider neighbourhood. The last quote reveals a certain reflexivity about 'community', this male, in saying that he knows everybody but stressing that 'it's not a community thing' was resisting the normative use of the term denoting the 'traditional ideal' of community as it has been constructed from the past and unreflexively utilised by many contemporary urban managers. Overall, we found that residents tended to refer to a sense of 'being local' or 'neighbourly' rather than making overt use of the term 'community' when talking of a sense of belonging or of being embedded in locally-based and significant relationships.

Where the term 'community' was used by local residents or professionals working in the two wards its use could be categorised as follows:

- as place, geographically defined
- as social networks
- as a symbolic construct
- denoting shared characteristics
- as a motor for collective action

We shall discuss the pertinence of each of these in turn.

Community as place

During the course of our research the city of Salford was often described to us as a city where its residents are strongly attached to their local area and as 'fiercely territorial'. A number of people we interviewed suggested that this strong sense of attachment to local area might stem from the working practices of the Salford docks. The docks were an important local source of employment, especially within the areas which made up Salford's inner city wards. Different 'docker gangs' operated the loading and unloading of the ships and membership of a gang was therefore an avenue to employment. In turn an important link to becoming a member of such a gang was often based on an individual's place of residence, where kinship and neighbourhood ties were instrumental in gaining the chance of employment.

Whatever the reason this sense of territory pervades down to a very local level. The following are some examples of how that sense of territory could work at the very local level. In these examples territoriality actually worked to limit access to local facilities in both Oldtown and Bankhill.

- At the time of our initial round of interviews, Salford's only Jobshop was situated in the heart of Oldtown and continually found it could not attract users from other areas, despite its acknowledged success in matching local unemployed people to appropriate jobs. Bankhill, which suffered from many of the same unemployment problems was therefore to have its own Jobshop but already there were fears voiced that it would not be used by many of the ward's residents because it was to be situated in 'the wrong place' to the West of the ward, in a place which was seen as student dominated and peripheral to the majority of the ward's residents.

- A youth justice worker told us that he was surprised by one young girl's insistence that there was no chip shop in her area of Bankhill - when he pointed out a nearby shop which was across the road from her street he was told 'it's not in my area'.

- An activist from a local estate management body in South Oldtown which serves a few hundred houses in towards the south of the ward's main council estate, described the local youth as 'tribal', explaining that local youngsters do not expect to see people on their side of the estate who are not from 'their patch'. The adult population of the area also accorded with this sense of who belongs to their area. Any young people who did not live within the residences covered by the estate management body who were seen in the area were immediately identified as possible 'troublemakers' and treated with some considerable suspicion.

These allegiances worked at a level much smaller than that of the ward. Professionals operating in the wards of Oldtown and Bankhill drew up maps which portrayed different areas of allegiance within each ward. They produced what can only be described as a 'patchwork quilt of localities' dividing the ward of Bankhill which had some ten thousand residents into thirteen distinct areas and Oldtown's approximately seven thousand residents into eight separate areas. Some of these divisions were based on existing boundaries such as major and minor roads which intersect the areas, some around the planned and built environment, for example, rows of older terraced housing or a single block of flats might each constitute separate areas, limiting the concept of 'community' to very small areas indeed. This identification of areas was often mirrored by local residents as the following quotes reveal:

> This is part of the co-operative and is like a community. (Oldtown resident)
> The block is a good community. (Bankhill resident)

Community as Social Networks

Within the two wards we found there existed a considerable number of quite varied social groupings - from sequence dancing and scrabble clubs to local history societies and church groups. Some were long-standing;

one bowling club had been founded in 1933 and was still providing 'The teaching of bowling and a social gathering' to thirty members three times a week in the summer and twice weekly in the winter. Furthermore when we invited numbers of people to focus group discussions we often found that the people we had invited were part of the same social networks, or had been in the past. If people did not actually know one another they often recognised faces and knew where other participants 'were from'.

Sometimes social networks and place of residence combined, as occurred in a permanent caravan site situated in one ward. We were told by one of its residents:

> This community here is very close, has never changed, won't let anyone do any damage, only mix with each other. (Oldtown resident)

More often, however, the networks were based around particular interests, age-groups or social needs, for example, mother and toddler groups.

Community as a symbolic construct

Where this idea of community was employed notions of belonging and exclusion were more readily invoked. We found more examples of this in Oldtown where both the homogeneity of the ward's social composition and the relative stability of the area meant that a shared knowledge of local myths and local boundaries could be more easily sustained. In some respects even to state that you are from Oldtown automatically acts as a symbol of 'Old Salfordian', 'hard young man', 'loyal to a troubled estate' and so on, because of the symbolic role which this estate generally plays within the city. Those residents and businesses wishing to distance themselves from the troubled nature of the place used a different postal address whenever possible, often removing references to Oldtown altogether. This was easiest on the borders of the ward where the neighbouring ward's name could be adopted. Within the heart of Oldtown itself a park was utilised as a symbolic local boundary where everything to the north was characterised as problematic and the area at its southern boundary was seen as 'honest Oldtown'.

This use of community did not work so easily in Bankhill. In that ward local connection could lead to the knowledge of which areas were considered unsafe due to high rates of property crime, and those which were safer, but this was a street by street assessment and said little about community and neighbourhood links.

Community as shared characteristics

Within Bankhill, ethnic identity played an important part in constructing community. A noticeable example of community constructed around ethnic grouping was that of the Jewish community within that ward. Jewish respondents did refer to 'their' community in a general sense, often articulating that 'it is different in our community'. But there was also a smaller Sikh community and an Islamic mosque in a neighbouring ward was a meeting point for many of the Pakistani residents of Bankhill. Conversely other residents of the ward often defined themselves as not being part of these groups, referring to these ethnic groupings as in some way different to the indigenous population, and as sharing a sense of community which had been lost to indigenous Salfordians.

In Oldtown being seen as a 'local' appeared to be the overriding definition of shared experience and culture and could become a method by which to negotiate individual and collective 'ontological security'(Giddens,1991). For example, one middle-aged male told us:

> I think ...[Oldtown] is a great area if you are a member of the community (went to the local school, grew up with the local villains, etc.) but terrible if you are an outsider.

Community as collective action

Within Bankhill we found a number of organisations existed which had developed around a collective concern and had formed their action around a particular residential base. One area had set itself up as a conservation area, another neighbouring area wished to follow suit and both had built up independent organisations to work to secure these interests. A group of Salford council tenants had joined with a similar group from a neighbouring city to work for improvements to their adjoining estates. Other neighbourhood and street based organisations had come together to try to deal with high rates of property crime and one had been successful in obtaining European funds to 'target-harden' all housing in the immediate environs. At one time or another twenty-eight Neighbourhood Watch schemes had operated within the ward. Not all of these groups were successful in achieving their aims, or in achieving longevity, but were examples of collective effort within the ward which had achieved some results and which (apart from all the Neighbourhood Watch schemes) were active at one time or another within the ward boundaries during the two and a half years of this research.

In the ward of Oldtown we also found examples of collective organisation but these were more likely to have been initially set up by professionals working within the ward, rather than having arisen independently as a result of resident action. There were exceptions to this, however. The ward could boast a long-standing tenant management organisation and a tenant management co-operative. The former had developed out of independent resident action in response to a perceived rise in crime and incivilities within one particular part of the estate. Its formation had also been prompted by a perception of police inaction. In a classic example of resident action a group of local people had formed a 'telephone tree' to organise response to crime and incivilities. If any resident who was part of this communication network saw a stolen car brought into the area, for example, the telephone tree would be brought into operation and some designated person would go out to deal with the incident. Some residents in this ward found an expression of community in membership of, or links with, less legitimate forms of organisation and especially in the local criminal network or 'Firm' which operates in different areas of the city.

Community in high crime areas

It was striking to us how often these different conceptions of community were linked to resident's perceptions of crime in their area. Talk of loss of community was also similarly linked for residents in both wards. These links are more closely explored in the following chapters, however here it is worth noting that in both wards crime and the fear of crime were both high on residents' agendas and were often the catalyst behind the formation of new community groups or came to shape the activities of existing groups. Of course people invoked the notion of community for a variety of other reasons and indeed the importance of crime was not equally felt in both wards. In Bankhill crime was first on residents' list of concerns about their area but for Oldtown residents the problem of having nowhere for their children to play was of primary importance.

However, the fact of crime and the fear of crime, held a

significant place in community relationships in both areas. Whichever form of community we encountered during the research period, its members had at one point or another turned to it in an attempt to organise fellow community members in some sort of resistance to disorder, incivility and insecurity. This resistance took different forms, sometimes practical and sometimes more emotional, for example in some instances people had turned to their understanding of community dynamics in order to try to place their own particular feelings and experiences of crime in a context with which they felt familiar. They could then use this knowledge to begin to make some sense of their experiences and to place them within a local context of crime which could make their individual victimisation experiences easier to manage. In these different ways local people could begin to find ways in which to make sense of and then to begin to 'deal with' their experiences of crime. There were others who were not tied into community in the same way, who did not possess the same depth of local knowledge, were less aware of the local context of crime and who therefore experienced fear of crime and victimisation in more isolated circumstances, but we found these to be in the minority. Most local residents had some measure of community which they could utilise to attempt to lessen the impact of crime on their lives. Without this recourse to some sort of community many of the local people we spoke to would inevitably have been more damaged by the experience of living in high crime neighbourhoods than they actually appeared to be. Community, therefore, however it was played out, could be used to beneficial effect and unsurprisingly the residents we spoke to living within these wards would look to utilise whichever of those relationships and understandings of their locality which they had any recourse to.

For 'urban managers' (the planners, the police and other professionals working in the areas) crime was also often a primary concern. Indeed dealing with crime (articulated in terms of the promotion of 'community safety') was stated as the main objective of the city's Community Strategy, developed late in 1994. Many community organisations and fora had been supported by this strategy and it was usual for crime to be high on the agenda of community based meetings. Indeed, in some instances 'the crime problem' came to dominate the meetings and, as such organisation is so often operated within local boundaries, it has almost become accepted lore that community as place is where responsibility for doing something about, crime is best sited. In areas which are multiply deprived and greatly affected by national as well as local trends this could leave community organisations feeling impotent to intervene successfully. In these circumstances a belief in the efficacy of the interventions of outside institutions can dominate and policies such as Zero Tolerance policing can become more attractive. We explore the efficacy of this kind of approach in areas like Oldtown and Bankhill in chapter four.

Writing the community safety strategy

Faced with the problem of high rates of crime and neighbourhoods in which local residents are suffering as a result the stated aim of community safety strategies has been to deliver planned reductions in their city's crime figures. Indeed the Crime and Disorder Act of 1998 expressly foregrounds crime reduction as its main target and enjoins local authorities to set specific crime reduction objectives. The Act advises local authorities to follow procedures which became accepted practice during the 1990s in those cities which adopted community safety strategies, informed by previous examples and a variety of guidance pamphlets and manuals (Home Office, 1993).

This Act directs that a city's or an area's community safety strategy should be informed by a local crime audit and the formation of a locally constituted multi-agency panel which can put into place the mechanisms by which the strategy can then be taken forward. Normally this crime audit has been delivered by an organisation outside the local authority - either a national body such as Crime Concern or Safe Neighbourhoods Unit or a local research organisation or academic institution. The body of data so collected has then been used to help shape a locally relevant strategy for crime prevention which has been delivered by local agencies working together with community groups and residents. Given this emphasis on local knowledge and experience and on local delivery mechanisms, it is somewhat surprising that the resulting strategies have often looked so very similar.

Of course it is true that many of the issues which concern one inner-city neighbourhood are faced by many others and that nationally felt problems are manifested at the local level. It is also inevitable that national concerns and priorities will affect local areas and will necessarily feed into local outlooks and attitudes. Furthermore, it is also increasingly recognised that problems which were once considered the preserve of the inner-city area can affect other deprived areas in rural locations or out-of-town estates. In this respect, therefore, the similar nature and concerns of these strategies, especially when they relate to similarly structured areas, is not particularly noteworthy.   However, it is important that these strategies do not miss the local dimension.   In particular, delivery mechanisms must be effective at the local level and it is here, above all, that a community safety strategy should include an understanding of specific local relationships as well as being able to address the wider concerns of a local area.   This emphasis on locality may seem straightforward enough to local practitioners involved in delivery services to a neighbourhood but in reality it entails getting to grips with an often complex set of interrelationships.   What is more, a focus on crime and crime reduction targets may serve to obscure differences between communities, rather than to illuminate them.

The centrality of crime or community?

During the 1980s there was a move to embrace the notion of 'community safety', rather than 'crime prevention', this move acknowledged the vital role of inter-agency co-operation in delivering effective crime reduction initiatives. Also implicit in this move was a recognition that:

> Just as the incidence of crime can affect the whole community, so too its prevention is a task for the community. (Home Office, 1984)

However, at the same time belief in the centrality of community in people's lives was waning in other quarters - note Margaret Thatcher's famous denunciation of society and emphasis on the individual - and within many local authorities an emphasis on community development was also on the decline.   So community safety strategies have also suffered from a lack of connection with the communities to which they are to be applied. Existing community safety strategies have often failed to key into the very specific dynamics of an area. This process involves more than an analysis of local crime figures and trends and of indicators of economic and social deprivation, but also entails gaining an understanding of the locality's social history, its position in relation to other areas of the city or region and its past history of community involvement. It involves an understanding that relationships within an area are not static, that they have changed in the past and will do so again in the future. Ideally it might also acknowledge that the neighbourhood may lie somewhere on a particular trajectory of change which has contributed to its current position as a high or low crime area and that this position can greatly affect the ability of the area's residents to respond to local interventions.

Currently, however, community safety strategies take quite a static focus when assessing the needs of the different client groups within a neighbourhood. The community safety gaze, and therefore subsequent practice, is informed by current debates which have emphasised the many different lived experiences which can coexist in an area at any one time and which are held by different social groups. So community safety strategies will tend to acknowledge the different perceptions of an area's safety and differential levels of fear held by the elderly and the youthful population, for example, or the specific personal safety concerns of many women and ethnic minority groups. The contemporary debates which feature, however, are often those which are nationally recognised rather than being informed by a particular, local experience.

The crime audits which inform local strategies, too, are often based around a display and discussion of recorded crime statistics as they are presented over recent time and geographical location. The audits' authors will often use these figures as the starting point for subsequent discussion of the prevalence and incidence of recorded crime as well as a discussion of the more hidden and less well recorded crimes (such as domestic violence and racial harassment) and incidents which occur throughout the area. This data is then likely to be supplemented by a discussion of how crime and the fear of crime affect particular social groups but many strategies again fail at this point to link these wider discussions to a particular local context. Community safety strategies which refer to particular wards or neighbourhoods do attempt to prioritise crime problems from a local perspective and then to proffer possible solutions which are then individually appraised, however a real discussion of community dynamics will more likely than not be missing and the Crime and Disorder Act's emphasis on the production of city-wide strategies may well exacerbate this trend.

A major drawback of this audit-strategy-options model is that its focus has been on crime, rather than community, and it has thereby tended to define an area's problems from a partial and in many ways static viewpoint - for example this approach may well demonstrate that an area is, or has become, a high crime area but cannot lead the reader to any greater understanding of the processes which contributed to this slide - and therefore can only present limited clues as to what can be attempted in order to 'rescue' the area.

Again, using our two research areas which will be more fully described in the following chapters, we can point to a number of examples of difference in the ways in which Oldtown and Bankhill residents perceived their area and its problems and which helped to lead us to our conclusions. Three of these differences will be discussed here:

1) Local residents experience of crime
2) The area's relationship to the city
3) The area's trajectory of decline

Although discussed in three separate sections, it will become obvious to the reader that these three sections are closely linked to each other and inform each other's perspective.

Residents' experience of crime

Although the recorded crime statistics for both of these areas suggested a similar experience of crime in both wards we soon found that this was not the case. The crime which took place in Oldtown was directly principally against businesses and new-build properties on the outskirts of the ward, or involved the driving and dumping of cars within the estate, but which had been stolen from elsewhere. So although residents might see crime taking place they were less often directly the victims of it themselves. A local criminal gang was known to operate from an estate in the heart of the ward. It operated under a code which was described to us as 'People don't take off their own'. Established residents of this area would tell us that they felt, in some way protected by this gang's code and told us:

> It's safe for locals but not strangers in the area

and,

> I've no real problems because I know the people and the area and grew up with the local villains and know local youths

This is not to say that all residents felt equally protected, and from all forms of crime, or that they wholeheartedly endorsed the activities of the gang, however they were aware that if they obeyed certain rules, especially that of not grassing, they could possess a sense of immunity from certain crimes such as the theft of their property whilst on the estate and much petty crime and vandalism.

In Bankhill, however, crime did directly affect residents' lives on a daily basis. In this ward there was no sense that anyone was immune from crime and there was a feeling that the area's residents had been left unprotected and vulnerable. The threat of criminal victimisation hung over, and greatly affected, the lives of all those residents with whom we spoke during the research. It was felt that this threat came from others living in the same area or street. As one police officer described it:

> The people in this area have no trust even of their own sons

Some community groups were forced to operate on a covert basis, only informing the neighbours whom they could trust of their planned meetings, and arranging venues outside of their area so that the existence of the group would not be discovered and jeopardised.

The area's relationship to city

Oldtown was considered to be an infamous trouble spot within the city. This ward received a great deal of media attention especially after one night of disturbances in 1992 which came to be characterised in the popular imagination as a night of riot. Partly due to this local notoriety and partly due to prevailing conditions in the area, the ward had received much political attention. Estates Action money was secured to improve the physical fabric of the locality and a prestigious business and residential development replaced the disused docklands. The area therefore stayed very much in the public eye, both as an area of regeneration and possibility and, coincidentally, as an area of decline and disorder.

The problems of Bankhill, on the other hand, went largely unnoticed and unremarked by the media. During 1992 similar disturbances to those in Oldtown were reported but did not receive the same prominence and attention. By 1994 however the area was beginning to gain a reputation as an area of high crime and disorder. It was included in a successful bid for Single Regeneration Budget funds in 1995 so that work could commence to try to reverse the area's decline.

In both areas community led residents' groups were active in the locality. In Oldtown residents strove to rescue the reputation of their area, recognising that a positive image was necessary to attract business and residents back to the neighbourhood. In Bankhill local groups felt that they must first fight to get the problems in their area recognised and onto the public and political agenda.

The area's trajectory of decline

Oldtown was an area which historically encompassed both disorder and difference. Its location near the city's docks gave it a reputation as a hardworking, hard-playing area of drinking and prostitution, but also as somewhat exotic - playing host as it did to visitors from all over the world. When the docks declined in the late 1970s and finally shut, the area came to be perceived as merely 'hard', somewhat removed from the rest of the city (not helped by its geographical isolation) but also as 'of' the city, an important part of its once proud industrial history. The reputation of this area is therefore inextricably bound up with that of the city in which it is located - this may well have added to the attention which it has been given. The problems of the area were seen as very much bound up with the area's economic decline, which is long-standing and has been borne, therefore, throughout the 1980s and 1990s.

Bankhill, at the time of the research, was a once-proud area going rapidly downhill. This area of large Georgian and Victorian detached and semi-detached housing, alongside smaller terraced properties, had shifted from being a desirable place to live, in which a 2-3 bedroom terrace would sell for over £30,000 in the housing boom of the late 1980s, to being an area of high crime, large areas of boarded-up, empty housing and heavily defended remaining properties by the start of the research in early 1994. In 1997 the houses in some parts of the ward are, to all intents and purposes, worthless. The only speculative interest in the area at the time of writing was from companies putting up cheap, new-build housing for sale on the periphery of the ward, or from landlords buying up some of the older housing for as little as £3,000 for a three bedroom property. The decline of this area, then is associated with the slump of the 1990s, a brutal and rapid spiral of decline, over which the local residents had little control.

The response of the residents in these neighbourhoods to their decline has been quite different and illuminating. Oldtown was seen by many of its residents as an area which had declined, but stabilised, an area where the local people, who have stuck with it through the decline are now best placed to seek solutions and control the area's eventual destiny. In Bankhill, the residents appeared overwhelmed by what had happened, in their very recent history, to both their investments and their sense of well-being. They looked to the statutory authorities, such as the police and the local authority departments to guide them out of their malaise.

The experience of community in Oldtown and Bankhill

While recognising that the experience of 'community' is not universal within each of these areas, in the light of these findings we characterised the two areas quite differently - as a 'defended community' (Oldtown) and as a 'frightened community' (Bankhill). In Oldtown - 'the defended community' there existed a perception of a negotiated stability and equilibrium and in this fiercely defended local area, crime too could be negotiated. In Bankhill - 'the frightened community'- no such possibility of negotiation existed. In an area where movement in and out of the area was rapid, relationships were necessarily more heterogeneous, fleeting and temporary. In addition, many of the old relationships and networks had been lost as those established residents who could do so, had left the neighbourhood in search of some stability and relief from constant fear of crime and acts of vandalism.

So different relationships of trust were found within the two areas. In Oldtown residents sought ways in which to manage their fears and anxieties, establishing relationships of trust where they could, hoping to find themselves 'on the inside' and thereby protected. In Bankhill there were few sustained relationships of trust - here crime was seen to come from within the community, and therefore alliances within the community to combat crime were more difficult to set up and maintain.

The case-studies presented here and more fully explored in Chapters Two and Three have been able to illuminate some of the reasons why community safety strategies ignore community dynamics and relationships at their peril. It has become increasingly obvious from this study that there exist very different possibilities for intervention and participation in different neighbourhoods. At an ESRC/LGA sponsored conference (Crime the Local Solution cited earlier) the then opposition

MP, currently Home Secretary, Jack Straw, suggested that national government might play a major part in helping to set local crime reduction targets. We go on to argue now, in more depth, why we feel this should not be at the expense of locally-determined strategies which can key into local needs and concerns while developing strategies for change which are acutely sensitive to the locality in which they are to be applied. However, before such an analysis can become meaningful to the reader it is important to set these two localities within the context of the City of Salford, and other similar areas across the country, as a whole.

1 Crime and Community in Salford

The 1991 census data returns show city of Salford is a predominantly white predominantly working class city, currently battling with the effects of thirty years of de-industrialisation in Britain. A century of popular representations of its culture - through Robert Robert's 'Classic Slum', Walter Greenwood's 'Love on the Dole', Shelagh Delaney's 'A Taste of Honey' to television's 'Coronation Street' have emphasised its white working class culture and often portrayed its people as living a marginalised existence characterised by poverty and poor work prospects. Yet at the same time these popular characterisations portray an essentially conservative city in which mainstream values and norms are largely accepted. Salford is not a spectacular city aiming to compete on a world-scale as neighbouring Manchester, neither could it be said to be a multicultural city, although there are pockets of difference and long-standing minority cultures within its boundaries.

The city is shown to be multiply deprived on a number of indices. A report by the University of Bristol (1993) measuring urban deprivation from the 1991 census statistics placed Salford ninth in its list of deprivation out of the 366 urban districts of England. The 1991 census showed that the city of Salford has low rates of owner-occupation of housing (52.7%) and a high percentage of its residents lived in local authority accommodation (35.2%). In 1980 the Black Report found that the city of Salford had the highest standardised mortality ratio in the country and although this improved during the 1980s the standardised mortality ratio still stood at 111 compared to 100 for England and Wales as a whole in 1989 (Salford Community Health: Beyond the Stethoscope, 1993). The social and economic deprivation suffered by many Salford residents can plays its toll in many ways. In 1993 the Public Health Research and Resource Centre, based at the University of Salford, replicating a national survey in two inner-city Salford wards, found levels of emotional distress considerably higher than average and the Salford and

27

Trafford Health Authority in the same year noted the overall proportion of smokers in Salford to be higher than average for the North-West region. The health of the city's children was also a cause for some concern - in 1991-2 Salford was 168th out of 181 districts for dental health of children of five years of age (Salford Health Authorities Purchasing Plan, 1993-4). One further area demonstrates the Health Authority's concern over the health of Salford's young - the low birth weight of babies in Salford born to young mothers. The 1993/4 Health Authority Purchasing Plan highlights this problem:

> Salford babies are more likely than babies in the country as a whole to be born to a younger, unmarried mother. In comparison with the North Western Region and the country, babies born to Salford women are more likely to be of low birth weight. (Salford Health Authority, 1992:21)

The concern does not stop at young people's health, Salford Health Authority also wrote in 1992 that:

> Salford men of working years, particularly teenagers and middle-aged men, are less likely to be in full-time employment than men in the country as a whole. This affects their personal esteem and the income of their family, which is strongly associated with its health. They are more likely than men elsewhere to die of heart attacks and lung cancer. (Salford Health Authority, 1992:21)

Of course, these bald statistics hide a great deal of variation within the city. This variation was highlighted to some extent by the Salford Health Authority in its 1993/4 Purchasing Plan when it noted that:

> Differences in death rates and indicators of sickness between different communities in Salford are associated with differences in economic circumstances. For example the population of Ordsall, in the inner city, experiences endemic ill-health. Worsley, in contrast, is an affluent suburb with residents whose health is relatively good. (Salford Health Authority, 1992:20)

These statistics adequately demonstrate the serious problems faced by health and welfare practitioners in the city.

The Post-War Economy of Salford

The traditional industries of Salford have been mining, cotton, docks and engineering, which later developed into electrical engineering. The opening of the Manchester Ship Canal in 1894 had 'brought the sea to Manchester' and regenerated an area of the city which had suffered from widespread unemployment and the closure of factories - over twelve thousand jobs were lost through such closures in Manchester in 1893 alone (Middleton, 1991). The building of the docks turned that area around, however, and at one time in the 1950s, three thousand were employed as dockers handling eighteen million tonnes of cargo annually (Satwiko, 1992). Much of this cargo supported local industry and when the docks finally closed on 30th September 1972 the impact on the city was serious. Job losses in the city were already far above the national average at the time. Between 1959 and 1972, 100,000 jobs were lost to local people and local men were hit the hardest (86,000 of these jobs had been held by men). This rate of job loss represents an annual decline of 8%(11 % for men) compared with an annual national job loss of one per cent and a regional loss of just over 6 % annually (GMC County Structure Plan, 1992). This decline led to Intermediate Area Status being conferred on the area by the national government in 1972. Prior to this the area had been seen as prosperous and was excluded from regional assistance grants (ibid).

1981 saw the formation of the Salford and Trafford Park Enterprise Zone, one of eleven areas so designated by the government in 1981. The creation of these zones signalled a move in government thinking away from placing the responsibility for economic regeneration initiatives on local authorities and towards the greater involvement of the private sector. These zones were administered by the local authority but were to place an emphasis on the private sector as a catalyst for change. They were designed to combat economic decline, creating additional employment and improving the physical and environmental fabric of the areas where they were active. Substantial incentives such as tax relief and lower rents were offered to firms to locate in the designated areas. The Salford and Trafford Park Enterprise Zone was locally controversial from the start. A local authority backed Docks District Plan had already been planned for the area covered by the new Enterprise Zone. It had the backing of the local community and had been widely consulted upon. The new Zone superceded this plan, and was seen to be an imposition from central government.   A petition organised by the Weaste Docks and Ordsall Joint Action Group produced one thousand signatures and a local residents meeting in April 1981 voted unanimously against the proposals put forward by the partners within the Enterprise Zone.   Whatever the merits of the individual plans the redevelopment of the dockland area within Salford would continue to court controversy throughout the next decade and has continued to attract criticism from local people that it does not address their needs as far as both employment and housing are concerned.

The dockland area has been transformed since the mid-1980s.   In 1995 the area included an eight screen cinema, four hundred and fifty houses and 18,600 square metres of office space with 'a four-star hotel, cafes and bars, a marina and moored barge converted into a restaurant'(Caine, 1992), and it has continued to be developed as a leisure and hotel space.   Perhaps one of the most locally significant developments on the dock site has been the Lowry Centre for the Arts described variously as 'a millennium project', 'a load of bollocks' and 'a building that people will come 200 miles to see and won't be disappointed if it's closed'(ibid.).   This Centre will house the city's collection of art by L.S.Lowry and will include further gallery and performance space.   It typifies Salford city council's desire to provide landmark sites of regeneration whereas opposition to the centre demonstrates a call for money to be spent on what is seen to be locally appropriate and long-standing employment opportunities and services.   Opposition to the Centre also reflects the attitude that 'Salford Quays isn't for Salford people'(ibid.), an oppositional stance which we were to experience on many occasions during the course of the research.   Although voiced in terms of a criticism of the policies of the local council, this stance often actually represented a wider dissatisfaction.   This wider dissatisfaction encompassed various elements of people's which had combined to make people feel that they were experiencing a less satisfactory quality of life than previously.   People spoke of feeling less secure in their homes and less trusting of their neighbourhoods, less able to predict future outcomes for themselves and their families and less certain of their economic futures.   In these circumstances there was a strong tendency to look around for scapegoats and our research emphasis on the local meant that this was the arena most often in the firing line.

So both the economic and physical profile of the city's industrial economy changed dramatically from the 1970s.   The domination of the city's industry by few and large companies had altered by the 1990s. Career Service data in 1995 showed that a small proportion of the city's five to six thousand companies employed a large workforce. It was further estimated that seventy per cent of companies in the city actually employed less than ten people (Salford Careers Service, 1994). Neither were these replacement companies employing local people at the cutting edge of change. The local labour force in the 1990s remained largely unskilled and the educational achievement of school leavers in the area covered by the Manchester Training and Enterprise Council (TEC) remained low: as an illustration - in Salford in 1995 11 % of Salford school leavers left with no qualifications at all. Salford also had a very low percentage of young people staying on in education after the age of sixteen.

Local post-war politics

Salford could currently be said to be a 'Labour city'. The majority of Salford people have supported Labour in both national and local elections for the majority of years since 1945, and especially since its present local boundaries were set in the local government reorganisation of 1974, (although the Conservative Party was able to win back some support in the mid 1960s; Garrard and Goldsmith, 1970).) Since then the Labour party has dominated local elections. In 1993 Labour held fifty-two of the available fifty-eight local government seats in the city. Its various local Labour administrations, however, have not played a radical role in the history of Labour politics since that time. In fact after the devastation of local industry and dockside economy which befell the city in the 1960s and 1970s, the local city administration adopted many tenets of the Thatcherite agenda and earlier than other city authorities. The 1981 Enterprise Zone began the sell-off of some of the city's worst housing stock to private developers in the early 1980's when more radical local councils were still campaigning against Tory policies around the privatisation of local authority owned housing. As already outlined the regeneration in the 1980s of the city's defunct and derelict dockland embraced a culture of private development and the subsequent and controversial emergence of an office, leisure and residential development in the area has been compared to, although obviously it is not as large-scale as, London's own controversial dockland development - Canary

Wharf.

The economic and structural changes affecting the city as a whole have arguably taken their toll on particular parts of the city - the majority of which are often referred to as 'Old Salford'. These consist of Salford's inner-city neighbourhoods - rather than the comparatively suburban areas - which became part of the city after the local government reorganisation initiated by central government which took place in 1974. Both areas in which the research for this book took place - Oldtown and Bankhill (local residents asked us to anonymise the area, so as not to tarnish their image) are wards within Old Salford. Like neighbouring Manchester, the city is unfortunate in including far more Oldtowns and Bankhills than its suburban and more well-off wards. This means that both cities have a low tax-base and must cope with a plethora of social problems within their boundaries.

Of course the inner city has long been seen as problematic. Fraser (1997) has usefully identified a number of different ways in which 'those inner cities' have been discussed in contemporary terms: spatially, culturally, ethnically, or (potentially) any combination of these. In some respects these contemporary discourses about the inner city emanate from the legacy of the processes of urbanisation and industrialisation of the early nineteenth century which were then prominent within the city of Salford. Images of city life emerged from these processes which not only identified parts of the city as potentially dangerous (especially from the point of view of health) but which also characterised the people as equally dangerous. Here lived the pickpockets, prostitutes, the 'police property' (Lee 1981) of the nineteenth century: and that section of society labelled by Marx as 'the social scum', and in contemporary discourse as 'the underclass'. Arguably the Chicago School of sociology, exemplified in the work of Park and Burgess, added further weight to these images by focusing attention on social disorganisation and the concomitant social problems (including crime), encountered in the 'zone of transition'.

Indeed, the city of Salford has an above average incidence of crime. The city makes up one of the divisions of the Greater Manchester Police Force and, at the time of the research the division's crime rate was significantly higher than the national average. In 1992, for example, the incidence of recorded crime in England and Wales was 10,500 offences per 100,000 population, in Salford it was 16,660 and the 1994 Crime Audit in Salford concluded that:

the impact of crime in Salford is very significant indeed. (Monaghan et al 1994:3)

Working in the city

During the research process around forty professionals working in the city were interviewed and asked to speak about their perceptions of the city. A number of themes emerged from these discussions. None of the participants in this stage of the research made these claims of the whole of the population of the city. They recognised diversity in opinions and differences in backgrounds yet the individual's talk of the city's feel and history was often also generalised across the range of those interviewed and it is these more general points which are presented here. They are interesting, not so much because they can be proved to be true in any way but because they were articulated again and again and seem to have become part of the city's folklore and go some way to illustrating the city's 'structure of feeling' (Williams, 1977).

The culture of Salford

Many city-based professionals were aware of the city having an identity in popular and academic (mainly historical) literature as the 'home of the working class', however many found it difficult to talk of the city as a distinct entity. A number of reasons were given for this difficulty. The city was seen as a collection of different towns, with no distinct administrative, retail or business centre or core. On its periphery the city merges with neighbouring local authority areas and its residents in these areas may identify more strongly with those areas than with their own. In these circumstances an identification based on local territorial affiliations has developed based on specific area of residence rather than to the city itself. However, those resident in the inner-city Old Salford are more likely to celebrate their status as Salfordians than those in New Salford, who may well even omit the city name altogether from their postal addresses.

The city was said by many to be suffering from an inferiority complex, comparing itself to the more successful and internationally famous nearby city of Manchester. Indeed it was so compared as early as

1844 when Engels wrote:

> All Salford is built in courts or narrow lanes, so narrow that they remind
> me of the narrowest I have ever seen, in the little lanes of Genoa. The
> average construction of Salford is, in this respect, much worse than
> Manchester and so, too in respect of cleanliness. If, in Manchester, the
> police, from time to time, every six or ten years, makes a raid upon the
> working-people's district, closes the worst dwellings, and causes the
> filthiest spots in these Augean stables to be cleansed, in Salford it seems
> to have done absolutely nothing. (quoted in Roberts, 1973: 9)

Salford's early history and later development has been
inextricably linked with that of Manchester, its currently more well-
known neighbour.   Salford may have been a centre of innovation and
excellence during the early years of the Industrial Revolution but it has
since lost this claim and in many ways it has lost its separate identity too,
as the city of Manchester has taken over the limelight.   Perhaps as a result
of this constant comparison with its close neighbour, the dominant
discourse among those professionals interviewed was that of an inward-
looking city, with its people possessing many old values but also as a city
resistant to change. The city was variously described as having a sexist,
racist and homophobic culture running through it and as a city which was
protective of those seen as its own residents to the detriment of those
perceived to be outsiders. This outlook was seen to be of some benefit;
the accepted Salfordian, generating attachment and commitment to family,
friends and neighbours who are seen as belonging but to be potentially
damaging to the newcomer or those seen as merely passing through the
city, such as those who make up its growing student population or even
those working in the city but who live outside of its boundaries.
      It was felt by many that the local council shares in, and in some
way can be held to be partly responsible for, the city's inherently
conservative and inward-looking culture. Different examples were given
to demonstrate this point and consisted of various recounted incidences
where elected members in particular, resisted innovatory practices. This
outlook was generally referred to as 'Old Labourism' and precedes the
discussion of New Labour and Old Labour which the current government
has popularised. In this instance Old Labourism refers, not to the socialist
ideals and practices of the left-wing of Labour politicians, but to a
tendency to hold on to old tried and tested practices, not taking risks or
'rocking the boat' and resisting the campaigns which the then left-wing

Labour councils such as operated in Sheffield and the GLC in London waged against the onset of Thatcherism in the early 1980s.

Crime in Salford

The city of Salford is characterised as having a high rate of crime. Many people perceived the majority of crime in the city to be crime against property. People were concerned less with issues of personal safety, when walking through the city or visiting residents in their homes, but were more worried that their cars, or the buildings in which they worked would be vandalised or broken into. This was true of women professionals we spoke to as well as male. When personal safety did come up as an issue people were concerned about being confronted by gangs of young people so tended to try to avoid young people in groups. Both men and women said that they would not respond if young people in groups called out after them lest they caused the altercation to spiral out of control.

As much of the crime in the city was thought to be property crime, and theft of computers or computer parts was seen to be a major part of this crime, office buildings and schools were often heavily fortified with bars on windows or steel shutters. This made the city feel more intimidating and unsafe and a number of office and school personnel commented that the buildings in which they worked felt oppressive and gloomy as a result (cf. The Salford Crime Audit, 1994). Interestingly a number of local professionals said that they would prefer to walk around the city and leave cars back at their offices as they were concerned about high levels of car-crime. One local businessman we spoke to had had a lockable container such as those found in ports to store goods, delivered to his work place and that he would park his car inside it on a daily basis as it was the only way he believed that he could ensure that it was safe from vandalism and attempted theft.

Many of the professionals we spoke to were concerned that there was a widely-held taboo against 'grassing' in the city. In certain parts of Salford this had been taken to mean the act of reporting anything to anyone official and this could make some professionals' jobs very difficult. This issue of the 'no grassing' culture came up in virtually every interview that was held with professionals and all were concerned that their work could suffer as a result. Professionals working within the school sector were particularly concerned that this taboo made it more difficult to tackle issues such as bullying in schools. Outside of schools there was perceived to be a problem with witness intimidation and also protection rackets against businesses. The city authorities acknowledged the problem of intimidation and set up a Witness Intimidation Scheme which was widely publicised and has attracted a lot of interest from both within the city and from outside.

Community in Salford

The organised and formal community in Salford was seen as quite traditionally ordered by many of the professionals working with community groups. Throughout the city we found there to be a network of active groups, all of which were invited to join area-based community committees when these were set up in 1994. Many of the active community groups were based around tenant's associations, the formation of which Salford City Council encouraged in the early 1990s. Their membership tended to be dominated by older public sector tenants, often male, although there have been efforts to involve young people and to set up young people's forums where the interests of the younger age group could be heard and their concerns aired. However, unfortunately these efforts to involve young people in organised community groups has generally met with little success and the gap between younger and older community members appeared to be widening into a gulf for many of the professionals with whom we spoke.

On an informal level the community was said to work in a much more inclusive way. At the informal level of community organisation the work of women, in particular, was said to be key to the sustainability of many local communities. It was especially the work of women in supporting others through extended family networks and friendship groups which was discussed. It was at this level of community that important relationships were forged which could serve as essential sources of practical and emotional help for individuals living in difficult circumstances. These sources of support could provide childcare thus enabling women to seek paid employment, to provide informal surveillance of the streets and the property of others, and could also serve as a link between the generations.

A strong sense of neighbourhood was also said to exist throughout the city, where being seen as a local was often to be offered friendship and support from neighbours. The city was seen as incorporating many close-knit communities of this type, working to the benefit of the insider but which could also be seen to work to the detriment of outsiders. Many such communities had been dispersed during the 1960s and 1970s when much of Salford underwent urban renewal and old terraced housing was replaced by the high and low-rise system-built accommodation which has become infamous throughout Britain. To many the damage caused had been irreparable, however new organisations and alliances were in evidence around the city and many old community groupings and networks had survived this upheaval.

Salford as a 'typical' city?

Despite the obviously unique history of the city of Salford and the different collective memories and discourses which have developed as a result of this particular trajectory of development, what is striking from a dispassionate reading of the comments of these Salford professionals, is how many of the city's problems are shared by other cities in Britain today. The poverty of the city's residents, the upheaval in communities, the inter-generational gap and high levels of crime are all examples of how the story of this city matches so many others. The response of Salford residents to their situation may well differ from responses and solutions found elsewhere - and we go on to discuss differences within the city in some detail - however it is true to say that Salford finds itself grappling with problems which are being felt at a national as well as a local level. Twenty years ago the Manchester and Salford Inner Area Study placed the problems of this conglomeration's inner core in a context of national deprivation within the inner city. The authors wrote:

> At the heart of the inner city problem is a concentration of poverty, an ageing physical fabric and declining economic opportunities...many characteristics commonly associated with the inner area problem are concentrated in the inner area of Manchester/Salford. This report confirms that inner Manchester/Salford suffers from severe problems of social stress and economic and physical decline similar to those identified by the Liverpool, Birmingham and Lambeth Inner Area Studies.

The raft of problems outlined above, which certainly are a

characteristic of many areas within the city of Salford, used to be seen as confined to the inner-city (Fraser, 1997) alone, but as writers such as Campbell (1993) have increasingly demonstrated, during the 1990s such pockets of deprivation are as likely to be found in the semi-rural or 'out of town' new towns and estates, built in the 1960s as solutions to those very problems which were first identified, and became synonymous with, the inner cities. Lack of investment in the physical fabric of these new places, declining economic opportunities, and growing poverty for their residents have also combined elsewhere in places in which similar social problems have been created. The troubled and excluded outlying estates in Oxford, Cardiff and Tyneside which Campbell describes as erupting into violence in 1991 are remarkably similar in many important respects to those inner city areas around England which faced similar disturbances during that period. These were poor, predominantly white, marginalised areas struggling with the effects of de-industrialisation and the subsequent loss of permanent job opportunities for the male work-force in particular. Campbell demonstrates how, lacking the traditional, collective arenas for this struggle, these areas were also losing a sense of community and co-operation, and, following the dominant discourses of the eighties and nineties were turning to individual solutions to their problems, such as crime. The effects of these solutions have often been extremely destructive, both of the neighbourhoods in which they have been applied, and of those individuals who have engaged in them.

General dissatisfaction in England currently appears to be quite wide-ranging. According to a recent report from the Joseph Rowntree Foundation (1998) just over one quarter of households in England report at least one problem with their neighbourhood which they considered to be serious (the four most often cited problems were crime, dogs, leisure facilities, and vandalism. Moreover, crime was found to be 'the most widespread source of neighbourhood dissatisfaction'. The same report states that almost 10% of householders in England identified four or more serious problems within their neighbourhood. According to the authors, however, these levels of dissatisfaction are not found equally distributed across all social groupings, they are instead:

> ... profoundly and starkly socially and spatially patterned. (Joseph Rowntree Foundation 1998)

The report goes on to describe the areas which express the highest levels of neighbourhood dissatisfaction as:

> ....wards characterised in official classifications as: social housing;
> deprived industrial areas with heavy industry; inner London;
> cosmopolitan London; deprived industrial areas with large minority
> ethnic populations; and areas of low amenity housing in deprived city
> areas. (Joseph Rowntree Foundation 1998)

It is well recognised that officially recorded crime rates, national and local victimisation surveys, all indicate that criminal victimisation is a key problem in these areas. The chances of becoming a victim for the first time, the chances of becoming a repeat victim, and the material impact of that victimisation, is likely to be far greater. Data such as these add further fuel to the image of such areas as 'no go' areas, as the *Independent on Sunday* characterised forty areas in Britain one Sunday in April 1994.

Assumptions about these areas abound in academic, political and policy discourses. The image of social disorganisation in these locations, originating in the work of the Chicago School and perpetuated in recent years through the importation of the underclass debate and the ideas of communitarianism from the North American continent, and mainly still concerned with the inner city, is strong. From the first of these debates is generated images of people who are cynical towards official societal values (especially with respect to issues of law and order); hold distinctive norms and values and with little capacity for conventional collective political action (see for example Murray, 1990). This stance portrays the residents of socially disorganised areas as a threat to mainstream society. On the other hand the second of these debates accepts the fact of social disorganisation and argues for the need to restore communities with a renewed sense of moral, social and public order, reflecting a view that such processes are absent from existing community life.

One key message which flows from the empirical investigation presented here is the central difficulty of assuming that all socially disadvantaged areas are in fact the same. The data we present below explodes that myth. We follow with a brief description of the areas which made up the research focus. Aspects of these two wards have already been introduced in the discussion of community and community safety practices found in our Introduction. The following portraits of the areas serve to place the two wards in much more of a context. They offer an image of the physical and social fabric of the two wards and their historical development, which is designed to demonstrate differences and similarities between the areas, and also to alert the reader to their ordinariness. The ward profiles presented here can be compared to similar areas within cities all over England.

A portrait of Bankhill

The ward of Bankhill is an old area which first began to develop an identity in the 1850s. Merchants built their bespoke residences in the area, facing open country and parkland and some distance away from the squalor of the emerging cities to its South and East. The area boasted a high status and in the mid nineteenth century its residents fiercely opposed a proposal that the township which had developed should be amalgamated into one of these developing cities. However increasing industrialisation saw further housing development during the late nineteenth to early twentieth century and the addition of streets of terraced housing, many back-to-back, built for the expanding working classes. From a population in 1821 of 880 persons, the area became a densely-populated neighbourhood of 15,000 by 1900 (see Tomlinson, 1973). In the post-war period as the Georgian and Victorian housing to the North-West of the ward was deemed too expensive or too large for many of the area's residents it was, in the main, bought up by private landlords and later by the providers of care-homes for the elderly or the previously institutionalised.

A further phase of housing development was begun in the 1960s as part of the general move towards slum clearance. Local authority-led, this saw selective demolition of the worst housing and thinning out of the dense street pattern in some areas. The space created by the demolition was filled with local authority new-build, mainly low-rise with a few tower blocks included in the building programme. However, the areas of terraced housing which survived were still in need of some improvement. The era of clearance and the mass-building of council housing was now over and different solutions were sought to areas of housing blight. Three distinct areas of rundown terraced housing were declared Housing Action Areas and General Improvement Areas towards the late 1970s and early 1980s. In order to secure sufficient financing of these improvements central government now looked to maximise the involvement of Housing Associations and the use of Housing Corporation grants in such areas.

Three housing associations were active in the Bankhill area at the time and each became involved in increased activity, purchasing properties from private landlords and owner-occupiers who could not afford, or did not wish to invest in their properties. The share of properties owned by these social landlords increased markedly until in the mid 1990s almost one quarter of Bankhill homes were rented from housing associations (McGrady, 1994:18). From 1990 housing association activity stabilised with little new housing development taking place and a move to maintenance and some relatively minor upgrading of existing housing association and local authority stock.

Housing policy changed again after the introduction of a new financial regime for housing associations as a result of the Housing Act 1988. Housing Associations were forced to seek more of their development funding from the private sector and to reflect the subsequent increased cost in rents charged (Randolph,1993). Under this regime full-scale rehabilitation of existing properties became more risky and costly and was more likely to be deemed inappropriate in areas such as Bankhill where property prices, subsequent to the mini-boom of the Lawson years, remained stagnant or declined in the early 1990s.

The area does have a range of well-used facilities within it. There are local shops and public houses predominantly located on the main roads which dissect the ward and a small supermarket with a limited range of goods. There are a number of well-established shops catering for the needs of the Jewish population selling clothing, kosher food and there are a small number of Jewish-owned bakeries. There are places of worship for many of the religions practised in the area. The ward also has a library, health centre, community centre and swimming pool however these facilities are somewhat run-down or vulnerable to petty crime and vandalism. The youth club was declared unsafe after repeated attacks and arson attempts undermined the fabric of the building and it was later demolished.

This limited portrait of the ward of Bankhill shows it to be typical of many similar neighbourhoods, found throughout England in the 1990s. These areas started life as sought-after residential areas for the middle-classes, became downgraded to respectable working-class at the beginning of the twentieth century and have subsequently been gradually incorporated into the 'inner-city' as the well-documented post-war 'flight to the suburbs' gained momentum. The housing and development policies which have shaped these areas were designed to alleviate poor housing conditions, to bring much-needed investment into rundown areas and to halt their continued decline. However, continued economic recessions in the decades of the seventies, eighties and nineties have placed great burdens on such areas and many have continued to deteriorate. Furthermore, research published by the Joseph Rowntree Foundation in 1995 demonstrated how central government housing policy during the 1980s had the result of concentrating poverty, and therefore allied social problems, in areas of social housing throughout the country. Despite the continued deterioration and decline of these physically diverse areas, the policy-makers gaze remained firmly on the problem of the local authority housing estate throughout most of the 1980s and 1990s. Mixed tenure areas like Bankhill were left to fail with little comment and even less intervention until mounting social problems and especially concern around increasing crime-rates in these neighbourhoods, began to force a rethink.   Bankhill became the subject of a successful bid for Single Regeneration Budget monies in 1995 however the redesignation of such neighbourhoods as 'problem areas' has only recently been fully and publicly acknowledged (See, for example, the Social Exclusion Unit's 1998 report Bringing Britain Together) which begins with such an acknowledgement).

Yet the decline in the worst affected areas of Bankhill has been relentless. At the time of writing many houses which would sell for £30,000 in the housing boom of the late 1980s are to all intents and purposes, worthless. There are a number of streets in which the majority of houses are boarded up and empty with remaining properties being heavily defended, many with bars and grilles at windows and doors. Many houses and businesses in these areas display signs claiming that they are protected by a local security firm. The only speculative interest in the ward as a whole has been from national building companies erecting inexpensive properties for sale on the periphery of the ward, or from landlords buying up some of the older housing for as little as £3,000 for a three-bedroom terrace. Solutions put forward by the local authority have included the small-scale; for example, the gating of back alleyways, to the large-scale; for example, the demolition of the worst affected streets. This latter was originally resisted by those local residents who have stayed in these streets and have strong ties to the area, but was later supported as an option.   However the cost of demolition and compensation would have to be borne by the local authority which does not have the finances to carry out such a scheme. Some demolition will occur, subsidised by Single Regeneration Budget and Housing Corporation finances, but this will not stretch to all worst affected areas. At the time of writing the local authority were seeking private sector partners with which to co-fund a solution to the remaining blighted areas within the ward.

A portrait of Oldtown

Oldtown is a residential ward which historically housed a great number of the city of Salford's workforce and dock labour. It is situated in the once derelict dockland area of the city which was known locally as the Barbary Coast. This area attracted seafarers from all over the world alongside those activities associated with such areas; prostitution, drinking and violence. Thus, this part of Salford has a historical reputation for being tough. More contemporarily, the area has undergone considerable transformation as a result of urban regeneration monies alongside initiatives established by the city council to attract business interests to the area. Its back to back terraces were largely demolished in the 1960s and 1970s and replaced with system-built high and low rise housing stock. From the early 1980s the local authority embarked on a policy which saw much of the worst housing on the periphery of the ward sold to private developers. These hard to let units were transformed into owner-occupied flats referred to by many at the time as 'yuppie flats'. At the same time some residents in the heart of the area were engaged in improving their own housing through the establishment of Salford's (and indeed Manchester's) first housing co-operative.

Oldtown now has two distinct parts. One is associated with the relatively new and prestigious dockland development, and one is associated with an area referred to locally as The Triangle. The former comprises private luxury flats and housing developments alongside new commercial enterprises in an attractively landscaped waterside setting. This is situated on the other side of a busy four lane main road from The Triangle and is visible from all parts of this part of the ward. The Triangle comprises council house property, much of which has undergone and was still undergoing at the time of writing, a process of alteration. This area also includes some high rise accommodation and a small area of large Victorian terraces. As has been said already, from any point within the Oldtown Triangle the rather surreal skyline of the dockland development, referred to here as Canalside in order to maintain its anonymity, can be seen. As a consequence its presence is not insignificant to those living within the Triangle.

In more recent times the Triangle gained some notoriety during a two week period in 1992 when violence erupted between police and young people living on this predominantly council house estate. Shots were fired at a police vehicle and a local carpet warehouse was set alight. Further credence was given to this notoriety by The Independent on Sunday 17th April 1994 in an article headed 'Fear Rules in No-Go Britain' in which Oldtown was one of forty localities described in the following terms:

> How else would you describe an area which taxi drivers refuse to serve, where doctors are advised to seek police protection before making house calls and which the police themselves will only visit in numbers? What do you call an area where the majority of law abiding residents lock themselves in their homes in fear of a lawless minority?

Such depictions are, of course, caricatures as some of our research findings will demonstrate, but they certainly capture part of the public's perceptions of areas like Oldtown in general and The Triangle in particular. Though it is perhaps worthwhile at this point to offer some further comment on the nature of The Triangle.

As perhaps the label implies The Triangle is a geographically bounded area, which there is very little reason to enter unless you live there. This generates not only a sense of isolation but also a feeling of separate identity in the area.

> From Oldtown I think they think that you're either thick or bent - I always used to say that about .... Square, but now it seems it's all of Oldtown. 'Cause people don't understand why you stay. People'll say to me. 'Aren't you frightened of going out at night?' and I say 'No, I live there, why should I be frightened of going out at night?' ..... I walk about, course I do. My patch, you're not shoving me off.

As this quote, taken from a local oral history publication, illustrates, this sense of 'my patch' provides a very strong articulation of local identity though this sense of identity is not necessarily uniform or homogeneous.

The Triangle itself also divides into two parts, the 'top end' and the 'South end'. The boundary between the two is the park, with everything the 'other side of the park' symbolising all that is problematic about the areas for those living in the 'south end'. Indeed one 'south end' management committee was formed with the express purpose of ensuring that their area did not end up like the North end of The Triangle. Moreover we were told that young lads from the 'top end' call south Triangle lads 'lemons' signifying their lessor local status. There is, however, no straightforward geographical relationship between these expressions of local identity and where people actually live. The role of family and other networks can serve to supersede geography in this expression of 'my patch'. This combination of territory and cultural values provides an important foundation, as we shall see, to understanding not only the importance of 'being local' as a key to feeling safe in the community, but also to understanding the 'structure of feeling' (Williams, 1977) within this community around crime and criminal activity.

It would be difficult to deny that Oldtown, in general and The Triangle in particular is known locally as a 'high crime' area with many of the associated problems that such a label implies. For example, for the ward as a whole the 1991 census records an unemployment rate of 22.9%, a youth unemployment rate of 32.4% and a single parent family rate of 9.6%. Overall the census shows that 61.2% of the housing stock was council owned, 23.8% owner-occupied, and 7.1% was housing association stock in 1991. The manifestation of these statistics is focused within the Triangle, which alongside the historical reputation associated with the ward as a whole born out of its origins as a dockland area commented on earlier generates a fierce sense of loyalty to this area which permeates people's beliefs and experiences of their locality.

To summarise: Oldtown is a geographically bounded area in which 'being local' and family and kinship ties still matter, especially for those living in the Triangle. It is also an area with a public and a private reputation for 'toughness' which is rooted in its history. It is an area in which, despite the material changes introduced as a consequence of Estate Action monies, has changed little, especially over the last two decades; the highly prestigious enterprise and residential development of the Quays notwithstanding. It is within this socio-economic and geographical reality that the ways in which people routinely manage their experience of crime needs to be located.

Understanding the inner city

Presumptions concerning the lived reality of the inner city (for inner city we can now read high crime area) abound in academic, political and policy discourses. As was earlier suggested, the origins of these presumptions are to be found in the political and policy drive to assert some control over the impact of the Industrial Revolution and the concomitant growth in urban development. Added to these processes was the Chicago School's concern with understanding and managing the social disorganisation associated with the zone of transition. The image of the inner city as socially disorganised has remained, and some would say has been perpetuated in more recent years in Britain, through the underclass debate and the ideas of communitarianism in their North American forms. Each of these interventions have their different impact upon images of inner city communities. On the one hand the underclass debate presumes that those people living in such area are cynical towards official societal values (especially in respect to law and order), have distinctive norms and values and that they do not possess the capacity for conventional collective political action (see for example, Murray 1990). Consequently inner city communities and the social problems which they represent, are seen to constitute a threat to mainstream society. On the other hand the communitarians, as articulated in the ideas of Etzioni (1996) argue for the need to restore communities with a new sense of moral, social and public order, reflecting a view that such processes are absent from community life. In the light of the empirical evidence presented in the following chapters and in the Introduction to this book, we suggest that each of these views are flawed in different ways.

To reiterate: one of the central messages from the empirical investigations presented here is the difficulty in assuming that all high crime areas are the same. The two areas under investigation here are less than two miles apart, yet displayed very different ways of managing their relationship to crime. Oldtown, which we have categorised as 'the defended community' is a well organised, socially ordered area, in which unconventional, and in many ways illegitimate, mechanisms of social control co-exist with more conventional processes. The less legitimate social control mechanisms may well go unrecognised by policy-makers. Certainly those who are less in tune with the area's social dynamics, would have great difficulty in understanding the effect of policy interventions in such an area and in understanding the social forces which might well come into play and ultimately determine policy success or failure. Bankhill, it could be argued, more closely resembles the stereotype of disorganised and disordered community associated with the high crime area, and we have categorised this as the 'frightened community'. Yet these stereotypes lack subtlety and cannot encompass complexity and difference within the frightened community. The shifting sense of moral, social and public order which we encountered within Bankhill, while undermining residents capacity for collective action (conventional or otherwise) did not appear to undermine acceptance of official norms and values, nor the search for conventional solutions. High crime areas are capable of containing both communities, in the traditional sense, and 'lonely crowds' (Reisman, 1964) and in differing combinations at different times. The policy possibilities and workable interventions which flow from this understanding would do well to take such complexity and variability into account.

Part Two: Crime and Community Dynamics

2   The Frightened Community

One of the first reports published by the Social Exclusion Unit - 'Bringing Britain Together' - begins by acknowledging that Britain has, over the last generation, become a more divided country. The report tells us:

> ...the poorest neighbourhoods have tended to become more rundown, more prone to crime, and more cut off from the labour market. The national picture conceals pockets of intense deprivation where the problems of unemployment and crime are acute and hopelessly tangled up with poor health, housing and education.....In England as a whole there are several thousand neighbourhoods and estates whose condition is critical, or soon could be.(Social Exclusion Unit, 1998:9)

Traditionally those poor neighbourhoods which have been labelled as 'problem estates', have been typified as the local authority built housing estate. It has been suggested that both the poor design and cheap materials used to build these estates have been a major cause of their social and physical decline (see Ward, 1985 and Coleman, 1990). The Social Exclusion Unit report quoted above, however, asserts that the deprived neighbourhoods which are the source of concern within this report may just as easily be traditional housing areas with predominantly privately-owned   housing.   These are areas which have been disproportionately affected by larger structural changes such as the demise of traditional industries and rising male and youth unemployment. As the report stresses there are thousands such neighbourhoods dotted throughout Britain, found in both city and rural areas. The area discussed here is the ward of Bankhill; its problems are not unique and in many ways they are typical of those faced by these thousands of others. However these thousands of neighbourhoods are also different in many ways. There are no 'off the peg' solutions which will work in all these areas. It is important to uncover the different nuances of local community and how social relationships are played out in an area in order to understand how best to engage with a particular community and to begin to address its needs.

Crime in Bankhill

Alongside the recent and rapid physical and economic decline of the ward of Bankhill, has occurred an equally rapid shift in the population's perception of the level of crime and criminality in the area. With few public buildings and scattered shopping facilities throughout the ward, the main victims of crime in Bankhill have been its local residents. Fully public buildings and scattered shopping facilities throughout the ward, the main victims of crime in Bankhill have been its local residents. Fully 79% of the Bankhill residents taking part in our household survey identified vandalism as a problem in their area, with 74% identifying crime as a problem. These residents were asked which crimes they considered had increased over the preceding five-year period and burglary, followed by theft and then criminal damage, were the most often cited. (From a sample of 302 Bankhill residents asked which crimes had increased in the previous three years, 196 cited burglary, 150 theft and 78 criminal damage). We found this local knowledge of crime problems to be remarkably accurate and these perceptions of the main crime problems in the ward to be borne out when compared with the appropriate sub-divisional recorded crime rates for the period of the study.

The effects of vandalism and crimes against property had stamped their mark on some areas of the ward more than others. A walk around the ward revealed some areas which looked well-cared-for and largely clear of rubbish and graffiti, whereas other areas were heavily daubed with slogans on buildings and sometimes roads, with back alleys heavily littered with burnt-out bins and rubbish. Some streets looked almost suburban and calm whereas others revealed windows and sometimes doors shuttered and barred or completely boarded-up. Many residents of these areas had placed broken glass or barbed wire on the tops of backyard walls in order to deter further or initial victimisations, although this had the result of further degrading their local environment.

Many of the residents surveyed had had direct experience of crime in the twelve months preceding the survey. According to the criminal victimisation data collected as part of the household survey, the victimisation rate for Bankhill was one crime for every two residents surveyed. In fact 37% of all those surveyed had been victimised at least once in the twelve months prior to the survey. Again burglary, theft and criminal damage were the main crimes committed against this 37%.

Bankhill residents were very aware of the localised nature of crime and disorder in the ward. Residents would routinely refer to the 'bad parts' and their decline, and the 'better parts' of the ward which had largely survived this spiral of decline and disorder. Residents in the 'better' streets, however, took little pleasure in this. The deterioration of areas close-by affected all research participants, fuelling a loss of faith in the neighbourhood and a fear for all their futures. This feeling of despair was demonstrated in the anguish of one female owner-occupier who had lived in the area for many years and who had managed to move out of one of the worst affected areas to a relatively peaceful street. She told us:

> The main problem is the houses, the houses that are being left, and they are being vandalised. Houses, beautiful houses that people lived in, what they expected to be their livelihood. They're losing it.

This feeling was articulated by another, male, resident who felt relatively secure in his area and who had had no recent personal experience of crime, nevertheless he believed everyone in the area suffered as a result of its decline, believing 'We are all victims of crime'.

Certainly fear of crime was found to be high across the ward in all areas surveyed, and was a major topic of discussion in all focus groups of local residents which were held across the two and a half years of the research project.

The problem of repeat victimisation is now well-documented (see Pease, 1991 and passim and various Police Research Group publications on the subject for an example of how this has been incorporated into mainstream crime prevention thinking). This can result in differential crime rates across geographical areas (Hope, 1994) or crime disproportionately affecting specific groups. Various explanations have been put forward for this phenomenon and they are discussed more fully in the conclusion to this chapter. Certainly in Bankhill there was a widely-held perception by local residents that some areas of the ward suffered disproportionately from crime than others. This perception too was borne out in police recorded crime statistics. A close analysis of all crime and incident data collected by the police for one four-week period during the research showed that certain areas of the ward were characterised by high numbers of calls reporting burgled houses, suspected burglars in residential premises, attempted burglaries and acts of vandalism to property and motor vehicles.

For residents of Bankhill the main causal factor for crime in their neighbourhood was not considered to be the design and layout of the street pattern.   Indeed residents in neighbouring and identically constructed streets could have very different experiences of crime and incivility.   Rather, local residents and professionals working in the area, attributed higher rates of crime in some areas to numbers of offenders, who were mainly young males, living in streets near to each other and influenced by the behaviour of their peer groups.   In turn other young people, less committed to offending but sharing the same or similar peer groups, could become involved in offending behaviour at different times. It was suggested that the more committed offenders might even 'recruit' others to help them carry out their work.   Younger children, under the age of criminal responsibility would be particularly suitable for the movement of stolen articles or drugs around the area.   Indeed this was witnessed by one of the researchers prior to the research project taking place when children around eight to ten years of age were seen carrying stolen goods away from a house.   An older youth stood inside the house at a broken side door handing out pieces of electrical equipment through the broken panel.   It became obvious during the course of the research study that to witness such events was, although not a regular occurrence, not particularly unusual either in some parts of the ward.   Offenders, and young offenders in particular, were described as very territorial, sticking to particular places which they knew well and returning to those same places to commit crimes.   So the pattern of high rates of crime in some streets was established, these streets suffered to a greater extent, residents moved out, communities were broken up and the area's downward slide was then almost inevitable.

There was concern then that residents in particular residential areas in the ward had a greater risk of exposure to criminal victimisation. In addition, some individuals and groups of people were thought to be more likely to be victimised than others.   The strong sense of territoriality and the narrow horizons of many young people in the ward led them to cite 'outsiders' as likely victims.   In focus groups with young residents of school age, the area's Jewish residents, often Hasidic Jews who due to their customs and distinct dress could be easily identified as such, and students who, it was felt, generally did not conform to the dress and style-codes of the majority of young Salford people, were singled out and were likely to be classed as 'outsiders' and therefore liable to be targeted for harassment or criminal victimisation.   Indeed the more well-off area of Jewish residence north of Bankhill also felt it was a particular target of crime and introduced an American-style private security firm to patrol its streets in May 1994. This area's residents were particularly concerned that their property was being targeted on the Sabbath and religious holidays when it was known that their occupiers would spend more time in the local synagogues. In addition, towards the end of the research period the local University began to advise its students not to live within the Bankhill ward because they too, were alarmed at the number of attacks on students and their properties in this area.

The adult residents of the ward, however, were more likely to believe that no-one was immune from crime and there was a feeling that the area's residents had been left unprotected and vulnerable. The threat of criminal victimisation hung over, and greatly affected the lives of all those residents to whom we spoke in the course of the research.

Community in Bankhill

Despite the sustained problems associated with the area, Bankhill had retained its reputation as a desirable area and a step-up from the worst inner-city neighbourhoods well into the latter part of this century. Indeed immediately to the north of the ward, within the area of predominantly Jewish settlement the suburban lifestyle is played out behind the tree-lined streetscapes, well-manicured front gardens and often gated residences of the affluent Jewish middle-classes. This area of Jewish settlement currently encroaches into the Bankhill ward itself where the less wealthy, but often large families of the orthodox and Hasidic Jewry have taken advantage of the well-built and quite spacious, but considerably cheaper, nearby areas of late Edwardian garden-fronted terraces to set up home. In contrast the housing to the South and the East of the ward is altogether more proletarian and basic. It consists predominantly of terraced properties opening directly onto the street. This area is characterised by housing association, private rental and owner-occupation.

The picture of Bankhill as an affluent area, a good place to live with a largely stable community and few problems, continued to be held by residents of the larger city until the end of the 1980s. Early in the 1990s however, well publicised disturbances took place across the country in many areas previously thought of as respectable working class communities (see Campbell 1993 for an account of events which took place in some of these estates). Bankhill also experienced minor disturbances, but these were barely noted by the local and regional press. By 1994, however the area had gained a reputation as high-crime and problematic.

At the time in which the field research for this study was taking place, around 10,000 people lived in the Bankhill ward. In comparison with other city wards the 1991 census returns showed Bankhill as having a relatively low proportion of people over pensionable age, but a high proportion of residents between the ages of sixteen and twenty-five. The 1991 census also showed a high proportion of lone parents and larger families in the ward. These census returns alone would show the ward to be disadvantaged on a number of measures. Statistics show, for example, that car ownership in the ward is amongst the lowest and unemployment higher than average for the whole city. Health indicators also show cause for concern. Figures supplied by the local Social services office in 1995, for example, showed the ward to have the highest death rate from lung cancer for those residents under sixty-five when compared across all city wards. Health statistics also showed the ward to have a high incidence of long-term illness across its population and the highest rate of chest infections and gastroenteritis in children within the city. Statistics also showed Bankhill to have a high incidence of child pedestrian casualties.

Census figures for 1991 showed the population of Bankhill, although predominantly white, had a higher proportion of ethnic minority groups than anywhere else in the city. The population of the ward included Jewish, Irish, Sikh, Pakistani and African-Caribbean peoples at the time of the research. Taken together, then, these statistics show the population of the ward and its surrounding areas to be quite diverse, both economically and culturally. Within this diversity lies the question of community and its salience for local residents. A more detailed exploration of this term and in particular its relevance to criminological literature has already been conducted in our introduction. What is outlined in this section is the particular articulation of community which arose from discussions with local people.

However the term 'community' is in practice defined, use of the term involves an acknowledgement of the existence of some sort of relationship of trust between a community's members. Local residents in Bankhill sought such relationships and used these to aid their management of crime and the fear of crime. The term 'community' itself was little used among local people - with the exception of Jewish respondents in the North of the ward. In this area over one third of residents described their area as having 'a community feel'. The Jewish community was seen by its members as close-knit, traditional and that community members knew and could trust one another as they shared the same moral values and the same religious beliefs which shaped their lives. Furthermore, it was generally acknowledged that fear of crime was lower in that part of the ward as a result.

Those outside the Jewish community also recognised its sense of togetherness and the community spirit which was engendered within that group. Many older residents saw in this community echoes of the Bankhill of another era when local people trusted, left their doors open to all and 'the rent money on the side' with the knowledge that this would only be picked up by the rent collectors. One middle-aged man who had lived in the city all his life, and in Bankhill for more than fifteen years articulated this sense of decline in community feeling. He spoke of how, in the past, Bankhill had appeared a very different sort of place, comparing the Bankhill of contemporary experience with that of his recent memory. He remembered:

> [Bankhill was] A super community. A neighbourly community, where you could go and talk to a neighbour. Now you knock on a neighbour's door and they think it's somebody bloody robbing, and they peep through the curtains.

Although over one half of the residents surveyed in Bankhill said that most of their family and friends lived locally, the term 'community' was not often invoked by the area's non-Jewish residents. In the non-Jewish parts of the ward the term 'friendly' was used to describe the local area by around one-third of residents. In the absence of the more formal and the family-based networks in existence in the Jewish area, local people in the rest of the ward looked to build relationships of trust on whatever basis they could be sustained.

In discussing the effect of criminal victimisation with the area's residents it became apparent that some of the worst effects appeared to result from crimes which had involved a trust broken. It is possible that these incidents were so deeply felt because they involved the person victimised having to change the way they lived their day-to-day lives. Residents felt that they should question the motives of those with whom they lived side-by-side and shared public spaces. Local people told us of how they had had to learn not to act in previously accepted, open and trusting ways, to learn that to act in a 'neighbourly' way might be a mistake and might leave them vulnerable. So whilst looking to establish trusting relationships, local residents were aware that this was fraught with difficulty. The answer, for many, was to fall back on tried and trusted friendships and their own families, rather than to build relationships of trust with newcomers. This served to further deepen the divisions within the worst areas and to isolate individual households from one another.

At the same time, however, possessing local ties and local knowledge was seen as key to maintaining a sense of security within Bankhill. Having local ties and being recognised as local by possible offenders, might mean being less of a target, and knowing other people meant holding vital information on who to trust and who to avoid. Many of the area's residents both adults and children spoke of the importance of friendship networks in maintaining any sense of ontological security. One group of women, all of whom had lived in the area for more than fifteen years, discussed how they coped with fear for their own personal safety by going out together in a group whenever they could. The arrangement which they had developed to enable this to happen had been prompted by an attack on an elderly acquaintance. One of the group told us:

> After little Edith got mugged, that started a lot of things in the area...some of my friends arranged that they'd meet a certain day every week and all go down to [the local community centre]. They're my age, or even younger than me ...

There was another sense in which local ties were valued in that they were seen as important elements in the maintenance of social cohesion. It was generally accepted that having local ties would generate a subsequent attachment to the neighbourhood and a feeling of neighbourliness. Good neighbours would keep an eye out for one another, look out for other people's property when they were out, keep streets and back alleyways clean and free of rubbish and were seen as an important element in ensuring the safety of the area and its community.

People without local ties however, often referred to as 'newcomers' were seen as less neighbourly. Bankhill residents often blamed 'newcomers' for the disruption of the once-stable community and, if not directly involved in crime themselves as helping to create the conditions under which it had flourished. This group were often characterised as 'outsiders' in the sense that they had no connection to the area and had not chosen to move there but had been brought in to the ward as a result of successive house-building programmes. According to this characterisation the first wave of 'outsiders' would have been decants from local authority estates in poorer areas of the city and the second wave would be housing association tenants brought in to fill the newly re-furbished houses taken over by the associations as a result of their inclusion in General Improvement and Housing Action Areas in the seventies and eighties. Housing associations were seen to have been more interested in filling voids than in ensuring a stable community could be sustained. The third wave would have come in to the area as tenants of private landlords seen as motivated only by an interest in making profit through renting to anyone who applied, without a care for the needs of the area.

Whether or not these accounts of the demise of a Bankhill community have any validity they are widely-held by many of the more established Bankhill residents. These accounts serve as a powerful explanation of the area's demise and as a cautionary tale which current policy-makers ignore at their peril. Indeed the echoes of such accounts from similar areas can be heard in the 1998 Crime and Disorder Act and in the rationale informing the parenting, community safety and anti-social behaviour orders as well as in the initial writings of the Social Exclusion Unit. Each of these accounts looks for a solution to problems faced by high-crime areas to modifying the behaviour of the individual community member, rather than to more widespread structural or cultural change. Paradoxically, these accounts are supported by those who advocate community action as an important element in the fight against crime. However by maintaining a focus on divisions within communities suggesting that there are at least two distinct groupings of residents which have little in common with each other - the good neighbours and the anti-social. The separation of these groups emphasises difference rather than community, distinction rather than cooperation and serves to keep people apart rather than attempting to bring them closer together. This approach emphasises the negative and anti-social rather than the more positive and social elements found in all neighbourhoods.

Knowledge of crime and criminality

Despite the problems which were apparent in Bankhill, more people considered their local area to be safe than unsafe. However there were three smaller areas within the ward where this was not the case. However across the ward more people felt that their area was unsafe than in the comparable ward of Oldtown, which featured in the research.   Not surprisingly in an area where over one-third of residents had experienced some form of criminal victimisation in the preceding twelve months, crime and the fear of crime were high on the local agenda. The nature of the crimes noted in the survey data and which featured in focus group discussions were typically burglaries, criminal damage and theft. Many of the incidents described by local people could be classed as petty crime which did not involve violence or high levels of financial loss but they nevertheless exacted a high price on the local area.   Incidents such as losing washing from the line, broken fencing or the theft of car radios, although minor, if taken on their own, were so frequently experienced by individuals, or those that they knew that the cumulative effect of all these incidents often had serious implications.   Many local people spoke of losing control of their day-to-day lives. Under these circumstances very little could be taken for granted - doorstep milk deliveries would often go missing, items left out in backyards - even heavy planted pots or hanging baskets - would be taken, cars had to be watched when being unloaded and expensive items be disguised or brought inside under cover of darkness, even metal drainage covers in streets and back alleys might disappear overnight. Residents spoke of being constantly on their guard and the toll that this could take on people's health and quality of life.

It was often the petty crimes like criminal damage and graffiti, so visible to the whole neighbourhood, which pre-occupied local people. A number of residents even felt that they found it easier to cope with a burglary rather than the constant barrage of incivilities and signs of disorder which they faced daily. After all an individual could insure themself against burglary or car-theft but not against the more minor crimes which signalled a neighbourhood in decline with an uncertain future. Stronger locks and new security measures could be installed by an individual to protect property and enhance feelings of security, but people did not know how to protect a neighbourhood under attack. Much of the crime occurring in Bankhill was simply outside the control of the individual. If grids and drain covers are stolen from along the street then residents must wait for the appropriate authorities to act, if houses are left empty, then subsequently vandalised, it is up to others to trace absent landlords or to initiate repairs; if graffiti is painted on roads and in public space then it is again up to others to respond. However, this general knowledge of crime and criminality impacts differently upon the older and the younger residents in this locality.

Older people: 'People round here have no trust; even of their own sons'

A substantial percentage of people living in the ward (over two-thirds of those who talk part in the survey) worried about groups of young people hanging about on the streets. Indeed this was one of the main signifiers of disorder in the ward, referred to on many occasions as a source of concern. Young people were closely associated with criminal behaviour. In many parts of the ward groups of young people (mainly male) are often very visible in public places. In many instances this is because there is very little for young people to do in the ward, in certain areas, however, these groups do act more like gangs and assert some measure of territorial control.- hanging around in large numbers and painting the walls, roads and empty housing with graffiti signalling their presence in the area. The graffiti in this area is often anti-police - naming and denigrating individual police officers - or pro-gang celebrating local groupings or individuals who are known offenders. At other times individuals are shamed as a 'grass'. These writings have the effect of sending out a very public message that particular gangs or individuals 'own' the streets in that area. Some of these young people will be involved in local house burglaries, others will be taking part merely for the thrill and excitement or out of boredom.

The link between young people and crime is firmly made in the eyes of many local older people. The sheer extent of crime and incivilities in Bankhill has contributed to a belief for many local people that all young people are people to be feared, avoided and mistrusted. In the perception of many local people young people are now 'the enemy'. In the words of one elderly female resident:

> We've reached the stage where we suspect children, all children and youths, and girls. You suspect them all.

This construction of youth as people to be feared has had an enormous impact on the neighbourhood. This fear affects inter-generational relationships and young people themselves are acutely aware of the fear they can invoke in older residents. Many older residents can see that young people are placed in a very difficult position as a result. They spoke of how the term 'young people' can appear synonymous with 'young offender'. Some older residents spoke of the involvement of youths and children in crime as an almost inevitable consequence of growing up within the ward as they become 'recruited' to crime by those they look up to. One woman, who had lived in the area for around forty years compared the situation to growing up in Northern Ireland on one side or other of the religious divide. She explained:

> ...it's like terrorism really. They're getting kids and those kids are being brought up [this way]. It's like the people in Northern Ireland that never knew anything else only war, and they grew up to be terrorists. It's the same with round here.

Another widely voiced point of view held that many young people do not become involved in crime, nevertheless, many who stressed this still preferred to maintain a wary distance from all groups of young people. One woman who held this view explained that young males regularly toured the streets near her house on mountain bikes, whistling to each other in codes. These teenagers were generally believed to be engaged in breaking into houses and cars, signalling to each other whenever opportunities arose or people were in the area. This resident had seen and heard these youngsters operating in this way as late as three in the morning and on one occasion immediately after her own car had been broken into. She was concerned that any local young males she saw might be a member of that group and she told us:

> When I see blokes on bikes [now], they might be innocent, but to me they're part of that gang, and that's who they are, and I do not like to see anybody on a bike.

Clearly this woman's victimisation and experiences had altered her perception of all young people. This was by no means an isolated incident and many others we spoke to felt the same way. This fear was very much a fear of local youngsters. People were particularly wary of young people who dressed in a particular style fashionable among young Salfordians at the time. These young people who engendered so much fear were seen to be local youths, often living in the same street. Indeed it was believed that the local knowledge possessed by these young people ensured that they would be more successful and less likely to be detected when committing crimes locally. This made local relationships of trust even more difficult to initiate or to sustain. One local police inspector vividly and accurately portrayed the situation in which many local people find themselves:

> The fear amongst people in this ward that you're pointing to now, is that it could be the next door neighbour that burgles you. You're not sure who to trust. When there's no trust amongst a neighbourhood, it perpetuates. They're looking over their shoulder and they're thinking, there's a fear ... these people in this ward have no trust of even their own sons.

In Oldtown local people can feel protected by their local knowledge and their acceptance as 'local people'. In Bankhill, however, people feel threatened by the localness of the criminality. Paradoxically to be local in Bankhill can mean knowing too much, being too aware of the local disorganisation and its possible consequences. In Bankhill local residents are watchful and have developed a sophisticated knowledge of the nature of criminality in their area. However, rather than promoting strong social networks, this local knowledge can breed fear and mistrust of others. In these circumstances a vacuum of neighbourliness has developed. This vacuum is open to exploitation and if not filled by legitimate authorities and social controls is open to others to fill. Indeed this was acknowledged by a local gang operating in a neighbouring area and as our research was ending moves were being made by this 'illegitimate authority' to capitalise on the social disorganisation of the area. Within a year of the research ending a 'security company' had moved in to the area and opened up an office in the middle of the ward, offering to keep a watch on the area and protect residents from burglary, for a fee.

Older people: 'This area is going downhill rapidly'

Many of the older residents in Bankhill had been witnesses to its rapid decline. More established residents throughout the ward turned again and again to explanations of that decline which were rooted in a loss of community. This loss of community was fundamentally linked to a loss of control and was subsequently more keenly felt. Larger structural forces such as the market, government policy, privatisation and recession were all implicated in the area's decline and all outside the control of the individual resident. One man who had lived in Bankhill for more than fifteen years told us:

> I can honestly say that on that road ten years ago, that you could get all your shopping down there. All your shopping. It was a community on its own. There was everything. All the people out. You lost this community relationship, community spirit. Now people don't want to know you. Like I said, you're knocking on their door and they'll think its either the police or somebody to fill them in, and they stay behind the curtains. Sad, isn't it?

Another long-term male resident spoke of the overwhelming feelings of impotence which have developed as a result of the area's decline and how individuals were often left feeling weak and powerless to intervene:

> The community is lost. It's lost, its wandering about because there's no back-up from anywhere. They [local people] avoid it. You get problem families on housing estates, you can get rid of them - you get problems in private accommodation, you can't. When they go on the private market getting private housing you can't shift the buggers. It's a hell of a problem around here. And people may look at it and.....they close their door to it.

This sense of a lost community, then, is seen to be rooted in a number of processes: the rapidity of social change, the changing housing market, the influx of newcomers with problems and not least in the response (or lack of it) to these processes by 'the authorities'. Local residents felt frustrated in their own attempts to maintain a local sense of community and an added frustration in the lack of support from those agencies which possess some local power. This frustration was expressed on numerous occasions in different ways in the course of focus group discussions - people exchanged strategies on how they might get the local authorities to act, blamed local politicians for ignoring their plight and attacked so-called 'do-gooders' and academics who were blamed for promoting liberal attitudes towards anti-social residents while having no sense of what it is like to live in an area blighted by their presence.

Whilst acknowledging the decline of the area, local people were no less loyal to it as a consequence. Many still held a strong sense of commitment to the area in which they had grown up, where their friends and family lived and which was so familiar to them. It is also true that many could not escape the area, even if they had wanted to, and this may have helped to fuel this level of commitment. However, many people had invested a good deal into the area - either emotionally, financially, or both - and were loathe to see their investment wasted. As one owner-occupier described:

> It's a shame it had to come to this. We never foresaw this at all. Most people, like me and Linda have done, they've bought their houses. You think you'll be there for so many hundred years. You might sell them later, go somewhere else. Your dream's going down the drain. It's not there anymore. You just don't know what's going to happen.

Despite their often-voiced criticism of the 'authorities' local people in Bankhill nevertheless felt that these authorities had a responsibility to act on their behalf to put the area back on its feet. The same views were not expressed by younger people in the locality.

Younger people: 'It's not so bad round here'

Younger people in Bankhill, perhaps unsurprisingly, do not express the view that their area is 'going downhill' with the same kind of vehemence. Focus group discussions with thirteen to fifteen year old school children revealed nevertheless that they did recognise the problems in their area and frequently discussed them. Vandalism, graffiti and car theft were the very visible signs of disorder and crimes most often talked about. Young people reacted to signs of disorder in their neighbourhoods in much the same way as the older residents and they were equally keen to live in places that were clean and free of vandalism and burnt out cars. They also recognised that their lives were limited in many ways because they lived in an area in which they were habitually confronted with crime and its after-effects. It was generally accepted by these young people, for example, that facilities such as youth clubs and playgrounds were not viable in the area because they would be routinely burgled or vandalised. However their attitude to their area was largely ambivalent. Whilst acutely aware of the area's problems young people had very little experience of other places which they could then utilise as comparators to Bankhill. Many had relatives and friends living in the same or similar places where fear of crime and the experience of crime were equally high. Young people were therefore very 'accepting' of the area's problems and spoke of how these problems were to be lived with rather than opposed. So many felt that 'it wasn't so bad round here' and displayed a fierce sense of loyalty and attachment to their area and to their family and friends.

Young people were also victims of crime. Whilst this research did not set out to collect rigorous data on specific criminal victimisation from school students, the residential survey did show that the sixteen to twenty-four age group in the area was the most victimised - with over one half of all respondents between these ages having been a victim of crime in the preceding twelve months. Much anecdotal evidence of victimisation and fear of crime was collected through focus group discussions with school children however. Male school students in particular worried for their personal safety, routinely accepting certain areas as off-limits because they were seen to be outside their particular 'territory'. Although all students found some areas more fearful than others - often linked to having seen stolen cars being driven at speed around the streets or because they were known to be areas where gangs of teenagers unknown to them hung out - it was generally accepted that boys were more likely to be in some sort of danger if they were noticed in areas in which they were unknown. As one thirteen year old male school student told us:

> What you can't do is expect to be safe if you go up the other end [of the ward] and into someone else's area.

and another young male in the same discussion group added:

> They expect you to stay in your own area so it's seen as strange if you don't.

In order to keep safe, therefore, young people stayed in areas that they knew or only went into other areas with someone to whom that area was a familiar and frequented place. Another much-used strategy to feel secure was to hang around in groups. Young people were aware that the locally held perception of young people as trouble-makers meant that groups of young people in the street would be a threatening sight to many older residents but they were not prepared to adjust their, quite legitimate, behaviour as a consequence. One fourteen year old female school student attempted to explain how she felt:

> All we do is hang about on the streets and that's what makes it better like ... a big group of us and we can have a laugh, like old people think we're ... and we're not hurting them.

These young people were, for the most part, far more concerned with the processes of managing their own lives in relation to other young people who belonged to 'the gangs' than in the impression they gave to others. How did they achieve that?

Younger people: 'Be known'

Young people repeatedly told us that the way to remain safe was to know people and be known, to walk through the area and note who was present on the streets. One fourteen year old male school student spoke of the need to be vigilant. When he encountered a group of young people he would have to 'check them out' to ensure that he was safe, he said:

> Most of the time you just walk past. But it depends who it is, if you know who they are. If their faces are known it's OK.

The young school students' advice to other young people who wished to keep safe was to limit their activities, not to cause people to notice them, to 'Keep yourself to yourself'. Many utilised these strategies themselves to ensure they were not targeted. All of these strategies reflect the routine concern that these young people had of how to manage their own lives without either getting into trouble with older people or 'the gangs'. Although this might help to ensure young people were not made victims of crime, it also greatly reduced their opportunities for self-expression and also had the effect of narrowing their perspective on life. Young people worked hard at 'fitting in' to be accepted, turning their attention in often negative ways to those who were in any way different.

People classed as 'outsiders' were liable to be seen as legitimate targets of crime. The definition of outsider was broad, encompassing notions of 'difference' but also of conformity to a set of normative values associated with alternative lifestyles and social classes . Outsiders were variously described to us as 'people who are stuck up', university students, 'oddbods' and 'straightheads' and even for one focus group 'men who ride trikes'. It seems that young people, in striving so hard to be accepted, and thereby safe, were absorbing quite narrow, sometimes bigoted and often reactionary views of other groups. This could, and certainly did, spill over into the articulation of racist and anti-semitic views.

In many ways crime affected young people in such distinctive ways because they were so very close to it. Many of the school students with whom we spoke knew others who engaged in anti-social behaviour or in committing crimes. They routinely shared the same social and physical spaces in which much criminal activity took place. Young people struggled both to occupy that space and at the same time to distance themselves from it. This put them in a contradictory position - on the one hand they wanted crime cleared up and their streets safer, but on the other hand they might also have had some sort of relationship with the perpetrators. This relationship did not have to be close but could still be keenly felt. As discussed earlier young people leaned heavily on the fact that they were known and accepted in an area in order to enhance their feelings of safety. If they were seen to condemn the actions of those who engaged in anti-social behaviour or set themselves apart from this group then they felt that they would be leaving themselves in a vulnerable position, open to intimidation and victimisation. When compared with the responses of older residents, there are self-evident tensions between the two.

Sometimes the school students we spoke to had quite close relationships with those who had been convicted of serious crimes. One group of fourteen and fifteen year old female school students spoke of a recent event in which a joy-riding incident had ended with tragic consequences - a local person having been fatally wounded when knocked down by the stolen car. Many of them, or their older siblings knew the driver of the car who had been convicted and had been imprisoned as a result. The group struggled to understand how their friend who was described as someone who:

...wouldn't do anything, he was dead nice and everything

had ended up in prison, responsible for the death of another man, a man who had daughters their own age. These school students therefore had knowledge of both victim and perpetrator and displayed great sympathy for the former and some understanding of the latter. They spoke of how many of the older boys whom they knew were involved to some extent in similar lifestyles and that it was part of growing up in the area for young men. They were adamant that young women were not interested in joyriding or committing burglaries, but that because many of their male companions and relations were involved, they displayed a grudging acceptance of their chosen lifestyle.

The role of Authorities

The rapidity of Bankhill's decline had shocked local residents and led to a great deal of uncertainty over what could be done to stay or reverse this deterioration. And it was not only local residents who were alarmed by the area's sudden decline, the owners of local businesses and many of those in official agencies involved in the area had been equally surprised by the turn events had taken. So, many people in Bankhill were unsure as to how to respond to the area's problems and were looking for answers.

Our research suggested that older people in the area still offered a generalised trust to the 'official agencies'. However the level of social disorganisation and high crime rates in some parts of the ward undermined a sense of belonging on which the potential for trusting relationships inherent in the call for help from the officials might be developed. The absence of social solidarity had led to a withdrawal from the processes on which such solidarity might be predicated. For younger people in this community the picture appeared somewhat different. They were wary of being seen to be talking to officials lest they might be labelled a 'grass' and this also affected their readiness to talk to any older people about their concerns. We have discussed how young people felt that to stay out of trouble of different kinds they had to manage the tightrope of being known (their mechanisms of sociability), not being a grass, whilst not being sucked into participating in the criminal activity in the area. For young people trust could develop between those who knew each other, but not much beyond.

Bankhill was seen by both the local community and local agencies as a difficult area to police. One of the main reasons which lay behind this belief was the problem of witness intimidation. In some areas of the ward many local residents were not prepared to challenge anti-social behaviour or even to report petty crimes because they believed that, if they did so, they would face recriminations. Intimidation could range from the seemingly innocuous - eggs thrown at the window - to incidents of extreme violence. We were told of threats being made on people's lives and the fire-bombing of cars and homes of those who were seen as working too closely with the authorities. In the majority of cases, however, people were concerned that their house or car windows might be broken if they were considered to have 'grassed'. One young Asian woman who lived in an area perceived to be one of the most unsafe explained the fear many people felt when they took a stand and reported any criminal activity they may have seen:

> When you've got to be a witness, you've got to get on the stand, you've got to point the finger. Everyone knows you and you're too afraid. You might have families, you might have kids. You've got a home. They'll set alight to your house. You're just too afraid to do anything. You just let them get away with everything.

Although this young woman lived in an area renowned locally for property crime and gangs of young criminally active men, a similar fear of retaliation affected people throughout the ward. Many local people thereby felt prevented from acting in a way which could mean they would be singled out as 'grass' or informer. In one area, we were told, people would not even put Neighbourhood Watch stickers in their windows for fear that their houses might be vandalised as a result. In another area local residents organised a covert residents' association. In this area residents' meetings would not be widely advertised, but arranged largely by word of mouth in meeting places outside of the area. People would not even travel to the meetings together as they felt they might thereby attract attention and be followed. This association became covert after those attending previous meetings were harassed and intimidated on their way out and one young couple, known to attend, had their house cleaned out of furniture whilst they were in a meeting with the police. While these examples are particularly grave they are by no means replicated throughout the ward. The fear of less serious intimidation was felt across the ward, however. Many people spoke of their reluctance to intervene in criminal or anti-social incidents. One male resident, who was in his sixties but very active and robust for his age, spoke of an occasion when he had seen young boys breaking into a toolshed in a local park. He watched the events unfold but, even though he was not alone, found he was unable to intervene. This event had left him depressed and more anxious than he had been prior to witnessing the incident. It had brought home to him how little control he had over his own safety and feelings of security and made him

feel older than his years and fitness implied. He explained the incident thus:

> There was a boy with a wheelbarrow full of tools. He broke into the park keeper's shed and walked out of the park with the wheelbarrow. There were about three of us standing there. We watched them. We were frightened to stop. I'm sixty-three, I was frightened to stop him. It was a boy of about twelve. I know he'll come back with his pals.

The difficulty Bankhill residents face in self-policing of their own communities meant that they were more likely to turn to others for help. We found Bankhill residents actively calling on the police and local authority to step in. Many, for example, called on the police to make officers available in their area more often and to be more visible - that is they called for more 'bobbies on the beat'. This was not an area like Oldtown where faith in the 'the authorities' has faded. Local people in Bankhill seemed to believe that those in authority were more likely to be unaware of their plight, rather than unconcerned. What is particularly interesting about the responses recorded in this discussion is the frequency with which people talked about trust.

Exploring trust in Bankhill

The concept of trust has been relatively underexplored in the social sciences. In discussing the question of 'ontological security' Giddens (1991) has argued that trust is most clearly evidenced in traditional societies through kinship relations, local communities or religious commitment. However he goes on to argue that the absence of these mechanisms in late modern societies renders trust no more than a matter for individual contractual negotiation. A similar argument is presented by Luhmann (1989). Gellner (1989) too suggests that urban life is incompatible with trust and social cohesion suggesting that such processes are rooted in rural, tribal traditions. Yet as Nelken (1994) has argued the questions of who, how, how much and when do you trust are central to understanding the nature of criminality and criminal relationships. What the data presented here also suggests is that they are central to community relationships. In Bankhill it would appear that such relationships are significantly mediated by age. The question of trust in Bankhill can be presented in the following way.

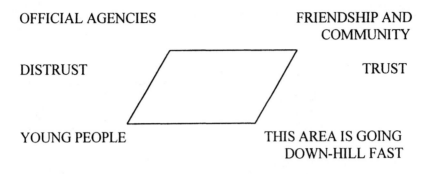

OFFICIAL AGENCIES   FRIENDSHIP AND
                                       COMMUNITY

DISTRUST   TRUST

YOUNG PEOPLE   THIS AREA IS GOING
                                     DOWN-HILL FAST

Figure 1   The Square of Trust in Bankhill for Older People

In Bankhill it is very difficult for older people (Figure 1) to create a balance between the four corners of this square of trust and hence some sense of ontological security.   The responses here appear to suggest that older people are still willing to offer a generalised trust to the 'official agencies'. Moreover, there are friendship and community groups which strive to offer some kind of militation against a totally atomised existence. However, the belief that 'This area is going downhill rapidly' and the expressed fears of young people undermine the sense of belongingness on which the potential for trusting relationships inherent in the call for help from 'the officials' might be developed. Thus there is an absence of social solidarity (being 'alright because you're local' which was found in Oldtown and discussed in chapter three) and a withdrawal from the processes on which such solidarity might be predicated. A key difference between this area and the findings in Oldtown (see the next chapter) For younger people the picture is somewhat different (see Figure 2):

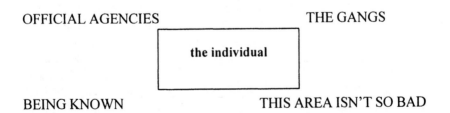

OFFICIAL AGENCIES   THE GANGS

the individual

BEING KNOWN   THIS AREA ISN'T SO BAD

Figure 2   The Square of Trust in Bankhill for Younger people

For younger people there is clearly a struggle for them to create a

sense of place for themselves within this community. They know they cannot be seen to be talking to 'officials', which for them might include older people. They also know that to stay out of trouble of different kinds they have to manage the tightrope of being known, but not being a 'grass', nor participating in criminal activity. For them, trust exists between those who know each other, but not much beyond. Their ontological security is finely balanced between these processes staying very much within the confines of being known and what they know. Hence the nature of the elements to their sense of ontological security (Figure 2).

The implications of thinking about the lived reality of people's experiences of high crime areas in this way are manifold, especially in understanding the mechanisms, which might underpin people's surface responses to survey questions. These implications raise fundamental questions about how we understand the nature of communities in high crime areas, the policy possibilities in such locations, alongside the continued relevance to talk in terms of the 'fear' of crime. Such issues are developed further in the Conclusion to this book.

Conclusion

So, Bankhill was a ward which, over the post-war period, in common with many other geographical areas of Britain, had undergone a gradual slide from being a desired place of residence to becoming a typically deprived inner city area. In addition, its residents had experienced a rapid and extensive period of both economic and social degeneration at the beginning of the 1990s which had 'tipped' the area into a steady period of decline, from which it was not able to recover. By the time of our study it had become known as a high-crime area, many residents who could leave had done so or planned to go soon and certain areas within the ward continued to decay, almost visibly, during the research period. Towards the end of our time in the field the responsible local authority had recognised, and begun to search for solutions to, the problems manifested in the ward and its surrounding areas. The commitment of the city council to work in the area alongside its existing residents was certainly apparent, however, at the time of writing solutions were still under discussion and the deterioration of some areas continued unabated. It had become an area of high crime, incivilities and fear in which residents were afraid to act alone to try to take control of their area, but might work alongside other agencies to attempt to reassert legitimate authority within the neighbourhood. In these respects, therefore, it concurred with the well-referenced characterisation of disordered place which has been described by Wilson and Kelling, in which:

> ...many residents will think that crime, especially violent crime, is on the rise, and they will modifiy their behavior accordingly. They will use the streets less often, and when on the streets will stay apart from their fellows, moving with averted eyes, silent lips, and hurried steps. 'Don't get involved'. (Wilson and Kelling, 1992)

In Wilson and Kelling's disordered neighbourhood people look to the police to provide the order maintenance which the community feels it can no longer provide, and in Bankhill too the community called for a more visible and community based policing style. However, the experience of crime and the fear of crime within the ward suggests that the process of decline in Bankhill has been so rapid and dramatic that reassuring though it may be, a return to an emphasis on a uniformed police presence cannot have the wide-ranging and long-term impact which is needed. Bankhill residents could indeed benefit from a period of respite from criminal victimisation in order to allow them to begin to restore lost relationships of trust and community, but it is questionable whether this will, in fact, be delivered by an increased police presence in the ward which, due to financial constraints cannot even be sustained in the long term.

The experience of crime in Bankhill points to a very real and sustained breakdown in community confidence; in the confidence with local youth and in the adult population that the area can offer much to them in the future. This loss of confidence comes from national as well as local processes and means that much more must be done to change the negative outlook which has developed among residents of such areas. The decline of Bankhill also demonstrates the shortcomings of the 'architectural determinists' who look to physical and environmental causes of crime and incivilities. This school of thought cannot account for the uneven spread of victimisation and incivilities across the ward, and is not able to encompass the contribution of community and relationships of trust which can mitigate the experience and fear of crime; issues which we shall re-visit in the Conclusion.

3 Oldtown: The Defended Community?

Crime and community in Oldtown

As has already been stated, as part of the data gathering process in this ward we conducted a criminal victimisation survey. From a population of approximately 7,000 people we interviewed 296. In the description of Oldtown which has already been presented in chapter one it is clear that the ward separates out into different localities. With the help of local people and professionals we were able to identify nine of these altogether. The survey of this area endeavoured to interview a representative sample from each of these localities so that we might be able to explore, in more detail, some small area differences as well as the more general pattern of responses to the questions asked. Some of these small area differences are reflected in the discussion which follows. In addition we conducted focus group discussions with residents, with 13-15 year olds, and police officers; and a range of other interviews and observational work in the area. All of these data sources differently inform the discussion below. The survey itself covered a range of issues only three of which will be the focus of concern here; people's expressed views of their community; their views of the problems to be addressed in their area, and their expressed concerns about crime in their area.

The question of community

When asked what it was like to live in Oldtown 16% (47 people) of our survey respondents agreed that their area had a 'community feel' and just over one third (101 people) agreed that it was a 'friendly area'. However, as has been already asserted, Oldtown breaks down into smaller localities in which perceptions and views of community were differently expressed. For example, in two of the localities in the south of the ward more people said that their area had a community feel (28 % and 27% respectively) than in two areas in the north of the ward (7 % and 8% respectively). Moreover, similar differences emerged on the question of whether or not their area had a friendly feel; 61% of people in the south of the ward agreed with this statement as compared with 21% of people in the north of the ward. As we shall see these small area differences permeated to a greater or lesser extent the perception that people had about their local problems and their experience of crime.

Overall, however, we met many people throughout the ward who were very active members of the community. Of 296 people interviewed the largest number (69) said they were involved in the local tenant's or resident's association; 31 said they were active in a trade union; 22 said they attended a local place of worship, and 17 said they attended a local mother and toddler group. Other community activities mentioned were Neighbourhood Watch schemes, Parent Teacher Associations, local history groups, and women's groups. However one of the most striking features from our survey of this area was the number of people who said that questions which were asked about feeling safe in their area did not apply to Oldtown. In fact people frequently replied to our questions around safety by saying that 'you're alright round here if you're local' or as one person expressed it 'you're regular round here'. The relevance of these expressed views is discussed in more detail below but they do suggest a view of the community which does not resonate with more public perceptions of the area and which arguably underpinned both the number of people who felt the area was friendly or had a community feel and were active in the locality.

The question of community participation was explored in more detail in focus group discussions. For example a group of women who had lived in The Triangle for at least fifteen years spoke of the benefits of living in an area where they felt they made a contribution and to which they felt they belonged. As one woman stated:

> It's the familiarity of everything isn't it, when you've been in a place for years, a sense of belonging to it. All my friends and acquaintances, and things that are going on, like we're all involved in trying to help make things better... I mean it gets you amongst people doing these things as well. I've made quite a few friends who have been involved in different things. They're very friendly-- Oldtown people.

None of these women had found it easy to get involved in the community at the beginning and they all spoke of being targeted for attention and/or intimidation from what they referred to as the 'anti-social' element when they had first become involved; yet, despite this, they had continued their commitment to local action. As one woman explained:

> We're all involved in the community... That gives you a lot of confidence anyway to sort of think 'I belong here, I live here, and I have as much right as they [the gang] have'.

Again the presence of the gang and the influence of intimidation is discussed in more detail below but it is certain that this sense of belonging within the ward seemed to help some people feel safer and more confident. However it is equally the case that those who did not possess such a sense of belonging may well have felt more vulnerable. Indeed, in other focus group discussions, some people did express such views.

This diversity of experience suggests the possibility of there being 'insiders' and 'outsiders' within the ward. Residents in the Canalside area in particular felt that they were not 'accepted' by the estate residents and that their houses and cars were more likely to be vandalised or broken into as a result. As one woman told us:

> I would automatically think that we would be much more likely to be the victim.... I think that ever since I've been here I've felt like a potential victim really and have acted accordingly.

So we were told that people living in different parts of the ward might be considered outsiders and indeed did feel themselves to be outsiders because of the part of the ward in which they lived. In addition, our data suggests, that all those running businesses in the locality also felt themselves to be outsiders, business managers believed that they were treated as though their businesses did not belong and that they suffered much petty and some serious crime as a result. As one managing director of a business situated in the Canalside locality told us:

> The local villains think of us as a sweet shop - they think they can walk in and take what they want.

This business manager said that he had never spoken to anyone from The Triangle believing that:

> We come from different worlds and have different agendas.

Those running shops and offices in The Triangle also considered that they were more likely to be targeted as victims of crime, even when they provided the community with much needed services. As one shop owner said:

> The ones we have most trouble with ... are youngsters who are learning their trade ... the older youths recruit younger kids ... help them to learn to steal and rob. They practice on the local shops.

In addition, whilst it is clear that some of the established female residents certainly felt confident and secure in their position in this community, there are some senses in which women felt themselves to be, and were also treated as, outsiders to some aspects of this community's life. For example, all members of the criminal gang in this locality were male and, as shall be discussed further below, we were told that if a woman offended the moral code of the criminal gang, then a male partner or relative would be punished in her stead. Women might be privy to information about the gang's activities but were not 'involved' in the same way as the male fraternity. Mirroring Beatrix Campbell's observations in her book *Goliath* women were more likely to be more fully involved in more legitimate forms of collective activity. Indeed, the police Field Intelligence Officer for this area told us that he targeted particular women as sources of information about criminal activity in the area. Moreover, some of the long standing residents and tenants associations derived much of their energy and activity (though not exclusively) from the women involved with them. So whilst we do not explore the gendered dimensions of this community's life in further depth within this study, we would wish to identify some senses in which women could be both insiders and outsiders to the routine daily activities of Oldtown.

To summarise: Oldtown, for the most part was felt to be an area with a good community feel to it in which people felt particularly comfortable if they felt themselves to be 'local' and were seen to be 'local'. This is a theme which will be returned to but it is sufficient here to note that this had the effect of marking some areas, and people within the ward, as 'outsiders' and this certainly seemed to take its particular toll on the business community.

Local community problems

We gave all the people interviewed a list of the possible problems which might apply to their local area. In Oldtown over half the people interviewed cited the following as problems; vandalism (by 187 people), crime (162 people), young people hanging about (152 people) and unemployment (151 people). The next most cited problems were having nowhere for young children to play (141 people), graffiti (107 people) and the lack of public transport to the area (106 people). Other problems were much less cited such as poor street lighting (46 people), poor housing (45 people), noisy neighbours (32 people), unfriendly people (27 people) racial harassment (23 people) and sexual harassment (cited by 16 people).

We also asked local people which of a list of possible crimes were a problem in their area; the most cited form of criminal activity cite was car theft and theft from cars, listed by 65 % of those surveyed. Other less cited crimes follow; 36% said shoplifting, 36% said businesses being burgled, 34% said drugtaking, 33% said homes being burgled, 27 % said criminal gangs, 18% said protection rackets, 15% said police behaviour, 13% said drunk driving and 6% said violence against women. So people were aware of crimes committed locally, however when they were asked which problems affected them personally more said they were personally affected by having nowhere for their children to play (37 people) than those who were personally affected by crime (35 people).

Respondents were asked whether they had been a victim of crime in the previous year and 23.7% (69 people) said that they had. Of all the crimes which people told us about which had happened to them in the previous year; forty were thefts of or break-ins to a car; thirty-five were crimes against property and thirteen were crimes against the person. Of course, these figures need to be treated with a degree of caution since it is easier for people to talk about some crimes rather than others and some events are more easily recognisable and definable as crimes. In addition, dependent upon where people lived within Oldtown, their experience of crime could be very different. It is at this juncture that the importance of locality re-emerges.

In Canalside and other areas of the ward, outside of the Triangle, people spoke of their experience of property crime as rather sporadic and treated such victimisation more as a 'nuisance' rather than as a major threat to peace of mind. In these areas it was felt that, although crime did occur, that businesses were more likely to be the targets of crime. In discussion groups in these localities people were likely to talk of taking preventive measures against crime in target-hardening terms, by planting prickly shrubs near fences, for example, or buying alarms, However in other parts of the ward the threat of crime and/criminal victimisation took on a different form. Talk in these areas centred on groups of young people, mainly male, who gathered in particular parts of The Triangle and who were seen to be involved in a great deal of anti-social behaviour. The theft of cars, mainly from outside The Triangle area, but driven and dumped locally, were a major source of concern for residents here. The experience of this anti-social behaviour generally seemed to be more unsettling and undermining to local confidence than the experience of property crime outside of the Triangle.

However, in areas throughout the ward, such day to day experiences of 'local problems' did not seem to impact upon the sense of personal safety possessed by the people living in these localities, but it was freely admitted that crime did affect the lives of local people in other ways. Oldtown residents as a whole expressed feelings of isolation. Local residents in all areas of the ward told us that they felt that, as result of the ward's reputation as a place where 'villains' lived and where outsiders were likely to become victims of crime, many people would be deterred from moving to or visiting the area. Moreover some were concerned that their own children would enter into the 'gang mentality', and that, seeing little opportunity for legitimate work, their children might become involved in crime. In addition local people also recognised that they had lost many facilities as a result of this reputation. We were told that local shops had closed because of armed raids and shoplifting, that delivery vans would only visit the estate before ten in the morning and that a local bus had been re-routed to avoid the estate. All of which served to increase the feelings of isolation within The Triangle in particular and especially amongst those who relied heavily on public services.

To summarise: crime did feature as a problem for people living in this ward but not as its exclusive problem. Other anti-social behaviour was also of concern as were issues such as having nowhere for younger children to play and lack of public transport. Again perceptions of these problems varied from locality to locality but arguably the general expressed sense of isolation experienced by people living within this ward lead them to look inwards for solutions. This issue is discussed more fully below.

Community and crime

There is another way, of course, in which local problems can affect people and in the context of crime that is through the fear of crime. The 1994 British Crime Survey showed that people worried more about burglary than any other crime and that people living in the inner city tend to report higher levels of fear of all crimes. We asked similar questions of our survey respondents.

We found the fear of crime to be gendered in Oldtown. In this ward women taking part in the survey did say that they worried more about a whole range of crimes than did men. Similar numbers of men and women said they worried about most property crime but significantly more women than men said that they worried about their personal safety during the daylight hours and when it is dark. In fact, men worried more than women about only one crime – that of having their car stolen. In Bankhill, where stated fear of crime was generally higher than in Oldtown these gender differences were far less apparent. So whilst it is not possible to directly compare these survey findings with those of the British Crime Survey it is clear that the gendered nature of the fear of crime in Oldtown compared more directly with that highlighted by these surveys. Women in Oldtown generally worried more than men in a range of different situations; being home alone, being attacked by a stranger, being harassed in the street, being robbed in the street; and in addition, when its dark they worried about walking past pubs and about using public transport. Though again locality was an important variable in these expressed concerns. Certainly in Canalside discussion groups much of the talk relating to the fear of crime was different for the men than for the women. Women in this focus group shared an experience of feeling threatened both inside and outside the home whereas a male resident of this locality expressed this view:

... maybe because I'm male, I don't know what it feels like to be threatened in this area.

But in The Triangle area most people talked about feeling safe most of the time. In this area, as has been suggested earlier, women are involved in local networks, perhaps based around their family or local commitments. Some of the women talked here of feeling uncomfortable in the park or the shopping precinct where young men do congregate; but other women said that they felt safe everywhere. This latter group tended to be those women with the most longstanding links and social networks within the community and who knew the young men hanging around. In the south end of The Triangle residents said they felt safer here than anywhere else in the ward. People here felt that the community had been able to take control of some of its problems (for example, young people had been actively involved by other community members to think about the consequences of their actions) and as a consequence expressed levels of fear of crime were much lower than elsewhere in the ward.

To summarise: whilst much is made in the general literature on sex differences in relation to crime and the fear of crime, it is certainly the case that in this ward this relationship is neither simple nor straightforward. It is clear that overall the women in this ward expressed worries about crime to a greater degree than the men but what is also clear is that these expressed differences were mediated by locality and involvement in the locality. Again the assertion of locality or some sense of local identity and belonging seems to influence how people manage their routine construction of well-being. Indeed, interestingly enough when people were asked in discussion groups who they thought were most likely to be the victims of crime and the offenders in this area; people in Canalside thought that people living in The Triangle were most likely to fit both categories and people in The Triangle thought this would fit those living in Canalside. The question remains, having become sensitive to some of the general features of the views expressed in this ward; how it is possible to understand them? How is it that what is publicly perceived to be a highly problematic high crime area is experienced by the people who live there in such different ways?

Understanding crime and community in Oldtown

As has already been stated, during the process of conducting the survey it became clear that the questions being asked of the residents of Oldtown did not resonate with their lived experiences of their area. As the qualitative responses recorded by the interviewers revealed, perceptions of safety in the locality were frequently informed by, 'You're alright if you're local round here'. This focus group work went on to validate this notion of 'being local' as a major theme which people living in this area appeared to employ in order to make sense of, and thereby render more secure, their routine daily lives. However, as the discussion above has implied there were other themes which underpinned the development of such management strategies. There were three identifiable themes in total; 'You're alright round here if you're local'; 'People round here don't rob off their own'; and 'I can't name any names but what's his face up the road will sort it out'. Each of these themes will be discussed in turn.

'You're alright round here if you're local'

As was suggested earlier, during the conduct of the criminal victimisation survey in this area people said such things as:

> It's safe for locals but not strangers in the area. (Middle aged male, unemployed, lived in the area for 29 years)

> Oldtown is a great area if you are a member of the community, went to the local school and grew up with the local villains, but terrible if you're an outsider. (Elderly female, lived in the area 11 years)

> I've no real problems because I know the people and the area and grew up with local villains and know local youth. (Middle aged male, employed, lived in the area for 35 years)

This view of the importance of local belonging was widely asserted in this research area by all kinds of people, and was reiterated in focus group discussions, viz.:

> It's like a culture thing, if you don't belong here you shouldn't be here sort of thing. ...As I say, I could walk about the estate, it doesn't bother me. In fact, when I go out at night, when I go walking round with the dog, I'm more frightened of dogs. When I'm looking round it's not for

> the lads or anything else, it's the dogs. I think the majority of people feel fairly safe in this area if you've lived here all the time. It's like S... said, you know who they are. (Middle aged female, established resident)

This view was, importantly, shared by younger and older residents alike, as one fourteen year old said when asked what advice would they give to a newcomer to the area:

> Get to know someone who knows other people around.

The importance of this kind of community attachment reflects a number of other aspects of living in this area. As the description offered above implies, Oldtown is quite a physically isolated area a state which is especially compounded for those who do not have private means of transport. But there were also close family and kinship ties which served to underpin this sense of local identity; a finding which resonates with other ethnographic research (Merry, 1981). As one member of a focus group with police officers stated:

> ...on the Oldtown estate, everybody knows each other. It's just like one big family, well not a family as such, but one tight community. A clan. That's it. (Male police officer)

Moreover to assert that you are from this part of Greater Manchester can be taken to mean that you are loyal to this part of the city and have a strong attachment to it, given its high profile public reputation. In addition, however, this sense of belonging is closely connected to the belief that you will be protected from being a victim of crime if you belong.

'People round here don't rob off their own'

Again this belief was asserted across the majority of localities and by different groups living within Oldtown; so people said things like:

> People don't take off their own - businesses are more likely to be hit by crime. (Young unemployed female, lived in the area most of her life)

> Teenagers here still have a code about leaving people they know alone. (Middle aged female, lived in the area for 33 years)

Criminals live here and rob elsewhere. (Young female, employed, lived in the area for three months)

But some of the thieves, they won't rob your house, so it's alright here cos they won't rob your house, or mug old women. (Fourteen year old school boy)

This belief was also expressed in this interchange between three fourteen year old school girls:

First:	No, but people who live down Oldtown don't nick out of Oldtown.
Second:	...look after their own.
Third:	They look out for each other.
First:	Someone from Oldtown won't nick off someone from Oldtown. They'd probably go down Bankhill to do it like Bankhill would come down here.
Second:	They don't mug anyone, they do big firms. They're not going to lose owt are they?

This targeting of businesses and the notion of businesses being 'outsiders' was commented on earlier and seems to have a significant resonance in this community. A resonance which some would argue is reflected in policing practices (see chapter four). These two beliefs: 'You're alright round here if you're local' and 'People round here don't rob off their own' were expressed so frequently that, we argue they amount to a 'neighbourhood dogma' (Elias and Scotson, 1965). In other words, they were not individual views formed in the isolated moment of an interview or generated as a product of the focus group process, but had a shared local currency beyond these particular contexts. The origins of these local beliefs are probably quite complex, but the influence of a quasi-political network, the Salford Firm, a locally well-known criminal gang operating in the neighbourhood, was undoubtedly one factor contributing to these responses and underpinning the final theme to be discussed here.

'I can't name any names but what's his face up the road will sort it out'

Assertions of this kind reflected an underlying understanding and implicit acceptance of Oldtown as a 'self-policing' community. An understanding aptly illustrated in this quote from a focus group with local police officers:

> It's always been a self policing community, always has been. But I think
> that is also a weakness in the community. They still dislike vandalism
> and they dislike most crime that goes on, but they are unwilling to break
> from the community chapel. The community is strangling itself, because
> they have to break free from old traditions, and the old, 'I can't name any
> names but what's his face up the road will sort it out. (Young male
> police officer).

Whilst for this police officer, not unsurprisingly, the idea of a
self-policing community was problematic, not least because of the likely
consequences of such activities for people living in this area, it was also
not without some benefits for those same people, as one resident
articulated:

> There's also a positive side sometimes. It doesn't always work one way,
> sometimes it works another. I've heard of a case a few months ago
> where a lad had broken these pensioners windows and he'd run off. Now
> a couple of people found out who he was, dragged him back to this
> house, and asked if it was him. When they said it was, they made him
> apologise, gave him a thump, and told him if he was ever anywhere near
> there again they would come back for him. Needless to say, he's never
> been anywhere near. It has its own rules as well. They sort things out
> their selves. (Middle aged female, established resident)

Such stories of 'sorting things out' have a long standing tradition
in this area and allude to the unspoken ways in which criminal activity of
a more general kind is less likely to be challenged. For example, one
retired senior police officer who had worked in the ward for over fifteen
years told us about one such incident when local people found some sort
of (double edged) solution to the problem of irresponsible joy-riding on
the estate:

> They [local young men] were then doing public displays of handbrake
> turns. ... In fact, there was one team who were doing it a lot and
> knocked three thirteen year old girls down. They were not badly hurt,
> fortunately, but they could easily have been killed. ... Eventually the
> people in the car had to pay £650 or make an offer. .... The other side of
> that offer is that if you don't take it you get done over for being a grass,
> so it's a bit like an offer you can't refuse.

These quotes serve to sharpen further our understanding of the management of well-being in this locality. There is a fine balance to be struck for all residents, young and old, between accepting the presence of criminal activities which people believe are governed by a code of ethics of a kind and from which the community might benefit (by receiving stolen goods, for example) and the knowledge that to offend that code, either knowingly or unknowingly, might result in an individual being named as a 'grass'. As one fourteen year old boy stated:

> But really in the end it's just best to ignore them. But if you really want to start trouble, grass.

The phenomenon of 'grassing', or more accurately 'not grassing', was well understood in this locality by old and young, male and female alike. Consequently it is worthwhile spending some time discussing this in a little more detail.

Understanding 'grassing'

The term 'grassing' has its origins in cockney rhyming slang. It stems from defining someone who is close to a 'copper' as a 'grasshopper', and was used in the criminal underworld of the 1920s. In its original derivation, then, a 'grass' was someone who provided information to the police about ongoing criminal activity, and, once an individual was known as a 'grass', they were certainly someone who was not to be trusted. However, in what ways is the term 'grassing' articulated and understood in Oldtown?

Key features of 'grassing' in Oldtown

Relationships between the police and the local community in the old City of Salford (that is, the City of Salford prior to re-organisation of local government boundaries in 1974) have always been somewhat fragile and tentative. In part the reasons for this are historical; as a traditional dockland area, it is a locality embedded in the routine practical relationships between employers and employees found in other similar locations (see, for example, Hobbs, 1989; Barke and Turnbull, 1992).

Moreover, Roberts (1972: 100) documents that in (old) Salford at the turn of the century:

> Except for common narks, one spoke to a 'rozzer' when one had to and told him the minimum.

Such unwillingness to communicate with the police has a strong contemporary resonance, as the following passage from a paper by the then Chief Superintendent of the Salford Division illustrates:

> First and foremost our thinking has been and continues to be informed by social and cultural realities of life in this city.   There are many complex factors at work which continue to provide the unique Salford culture, and I am only highlighting one or two.   The old 'Barbary Coast' may have disappeared with the closure of the Terminal Docks and slum clearances of the 1970s, but the docking community ethos lives on.   Not only in the old docks area, but wherever Salfordians, moved from the slums, were re-settled.   The docking communities had long endured harsh social and economic conditions and had developed mechanisms to help cope with these realities.   One was to remove goods from the docks for the use of self, family, neighbours, friends, etc.   This meant there was a certain reserve and reticence shown towards the police (dock or city), lest they should discover too much about the few possessions any individual had.
>   Therein lies the root of the modern phenomenon of 'No Grassing' which so powerfully influences social behaviour in this city. This today means far more than its traditional interpretation, as part of that so called Code of Honour amongst thieves, which purportedly prohibited an individual, brought to book for his misdemeanours, from naming his accomplices.   'Grassing' is now given a wider meaning so as to include any communication, of any kind whatsoever, with not only the police, but also all those deemed to be 'in authority'. (Cramphorn, November 1994)

Not only does this quote illustrate both the historical context to understanding 'grassing' in Salford, and its contemporary wider interpretation to include authorities other than the police, it also implicitly demonstrates the extent to which the police regard this phenomenon as a barrier to meaningful and effective policing in this ward (see chapter four).

The influence and power that the rules around 'grassing' wield are learned very quickly in the area.   As one female burglary victim -

interviewed as a part of a separate research project- and who had lived in Salford for less than two years stated when asked if she would report a crime to the police again:

> No - I've already reported cases seven times and it's not worth it cos they don't do anything and I'm worried about being thought of as a 'grass' and the victimisation you can get as a result of this. I don't always report now because they think you're a 'grass' and spray graffiti about you and bully you. (Burglary victim, female, interviewed September 1993)

Arguably, as we shall see, this woman's testimony needs to be contextualised not only in terms of the local cultural norms of not reporting incidents to those in authority but also in terms of the general belief that the police 'don't do anything'. Indeed, her relative newness to the community may also have been a factor contributing to both her inability to manage the events happening to her and the level of acceptance of her as a member of the community. Another feature of 'insiders' and 'outsiders' referred to earlier in this chapter.

Being a stranger, then, is problematic in relation to the phenomenon of 'grassing' in Oldtown. Indeed, a Home Office sponsored survey on witness intimidation was aborted in the area in December 1993:

> In Salford the survey was aborted before the end of the survey period because of threats to an interviewer and abusive behaviour to residents, known to have been interviewed. (Maynard, 1994)

The focus of this Home Office survey may, of course, have constituted what was particularly problematic about the presence of interviewers on the estate. The experience of those interviewers, however, certainly intimates the importance of understanding the presence and influence of gang activity in the area, as this quote from the Salford City Reporter (17 March 1994) also illustrates:

> The man dubbed Salford's Mr Big, --, was in court after being arrested after a 'brawl' at the Club 21, Piccadilly in Manchester. The prosecution dropped charges of violent disorder against him and eight others after the court was told that police had decided not to pursue the matter because witnesses were afraid.

The potential impact of the processes surrounding witness intimidation returns us neatly to the question of the extent to which this 'no-grassing' rule acts as a barrier to effective policing.

This discussion of 'grassing' so far has alerted us to a number of aspects to this phenomenon; there are however three key elements to this phenomenon which leads to its manifestation in particular ways. These elements can be identified as intimidation, politicisation, and socialisation. Whilst each of these are not mutually exclusive categories, they are terms which highlight the different ways in which 'grassing' is understood and harnessed in the locality. We will explore each of these separately.

Grassing and 'intimidation'

'Grassing' as intimidation has two dimensions to it. The first features in the official discourses of the police and other agencies in their talk of the area. It is given substance in a number of ways. Not only through the more eloquent analysis of the former divisional commander cited earlier, but also through the circulation of accurate or not so accurate stories of incidents and people in the locality. During the course of our research two stories were offered to us as being illustrative of the power of this kind of intimidation. They are presented here in the words of a retired Police Superintendent who spent some considerable time during his career working in Oldtown. In referring to the notorious carpet warehouse fire on the outskirts of the ward in 1992 and referred to previously, he told us:

> Carpetworld came about as a response to the police and the community in the area, trying to solve a particular problem of stolen vehicles being used against property in the area. But again to raise their own profile, to inspire intimidation and to create the myth.

> (RESEARCHER) Which part of the estate was that because it does seem to be one part of the estate where people constantly refer to the dangerousness of the speed of cars and joy-riding?

> The same people still live in that sort of area [---- Road], those three girls, initially the incident was reported to us - this is one of the area which you mentioned at the beginning where an approach was made from Mr M and some of his friends to intercede and sort the business out.

These stories allude to the belief in the powerful presence of a 'Mr Big', a presence which appears to inform the response of both the police and the community to the processes of grassing. As far as the police and other official agencies are concerned, however, this presence is always spoken of in terms of intimidation, and, as a consequence, as a barrier to not only effective police community relations but also effective policing.

It should be remembered, of course, that what we have identified here is a way of talking about a particular locality, the impact of which may vary according to which constituent part of the community is being addressed. For example, the Home Office study cited earlier interviewed 188 people in Oldtown, 23% of whom had been a victim of crime in the previous year and of that 23%, eighteen individuals knew their offender's identity and still reported the crime to the police, thus emphasising the significance of this talk in people's routine daily lives, rather than its necessary concomitant empirical reality.

However, it is through stories such as these that the police attribute a local lack of trust in them and therefore a subsequent unwillingness to pass on information. This does not mean, however, that individual police officers are not trusted. In different ways both the local Field Intelligence Officer and the Schools Liaison Officer who were working in the area when the research began, appeared to have good, individually-based local relations with some sections of the community. But despite these good relations, they too were not completely exempted from the second aspect of intimidation: public shaming.

In the middle of Oldtown was an area in which nearly all the local amenities were located: a supermarket (which closed during the research period), a chemist, betting shop, job shop, post office, public house and a hardware store. This area provided the physical location and space for 'public shaming' ceremonies to take place. In other words, if there was graffiti to be written, and if there was graffiti to be written about a particular person who it was believed had 'grassed', then their name would be likely to appear in this location. It was here that people were named for the rest of the community to see: and since this was one of the few places where there were any local amenities in Oldtown, and certainly had the greatest concentration, then it served its purpose as a public arena of shame very well.

The use of this arena in this way served a number of functions in the local community. It certainly provided a very real forum in which members of the local community were made very much aware of not only who had been accused of 'grassing' but also of the consequences of being so accused.   The desire to avoid such 'public shaming' was one basis on which choices of individual community members were made concerning who to inform about what.   Moreover, the actual appearance of names in this arena served a deeper function: it marked, potentially, those whose behaviour had been deemed outside of the locally accepted norms and values.   As such it served to remind all members of Oldtown of those norms and values.   In this sense, there may be a similar functional relationship between the processes associated with public shaming and the further maintenance of social solidarity and cohesion found within this local community.   Processes not dissimilar, perhaps, to those identified in Puritan communities by Erikson (1966).

Those held responsible for intimidating the community in this way were commonly referred to as the 'Salford Firm'.   The presence of this gang in the locality was widely acknowledged, both in official discourses about the area and in individual community members' articulations about their locality (as discussed above).   It is the nature and extent of this presence and its influence which can be disputed, but what is less in doubt are the aspirations towards political credibility associated with the gang's activities.   In reality this gang probably comprised twenty to thirty 'full-time' members, involved in criminal activity at varying levels of seriousness.   Understanding the political aspirations associated with these activities provides a different insight into understanding the phenomenon of 'grassing'.

Grassing and 'politicisation'

The relationship between 'politicisation' and 'grassing' introduces the notion of a moral code underpinning the processes under discussion here. This is alluded to and then clarified in the following quotes taken from an interview with the self-acclaimed spokesperson for the 'Salford Firm'.

> ... Cos a lot of people accuse us, saying that M..., you know, encourages them to break the law, but I don't have to encourage them to break the law, people who make them break the law are those who are responsible for them breaking the law, you know the councillors, the politicians - these are the ones who are responsible, not me. I only advise them how not to get caught, you know, don't do this, don't go robbing off old ladies, mugging old ladies - it's not on - you know, don't go robbing and

burgling ordinary people's houses of televisions, you know, if you want to go and rob, go to Canalside.

Moreover, we were told that when incidents occur which break this moral code:

> ... we try to find out who's done it and if they're really young people, then we'll given them a talking to, you know, to say 'it's out of order', you know what I mean, but if it's someone who's supposed to be, you know, responsible and knew what they was doing - knew that it was a woman on her own or a woman with three kids and no husband, you know what I mean, they get a smacking ... [this is] street politics, you know. It's not on - there's too many burglaries going on, we've got to put a stop to it, you know what I mean. We don't go and tell the police, you know, we've got to handle it ourselves, you know, there's got to be some kind of, you know, street justice, so when the lads find out who's going round breaking into people's houses, they get a smacking, you know what I mean, and it's called 'taxing', you know ...

These processes obviously give a very different flavour to the notion of 'community policing' than that offered by the rhetoric of 'community partnership' or Neighbourhood Watch.

The recognition of a political dimension to this gang's involvement in crime and its justification offered a different and arguably more subtle definition of what counts as 'grassing', which does not always mean not informing the police. The gang spokesman tried to explain their application of the term thus:

> ...You've not got to be a grass, I mean, there's a code in that - when is it right to inform the police about a certain thing, and when is it not correct. You know, if someone rapes somebody or interferes with a kid, or mugs an old lady, as far as the correct-minded thing for people, you know what I mean, the concern - if somebody hands them in then they're not grassing, you know. But if somebody goes and says 'so and so has done a ram-raid' or 'so and so has done a post office', then it's grassing, it's not acceptable.

So the processes associated with 'grassing', for those seen to be responsible for perpetuating those processes, possessed some subtlety, and were defended as not purely criminal but also as in some sense moral. Indeed, the subtlety of these understandings, permeated and supported some aspects of the views expressed by local individual residents in response to survey questions on perceptions of crime and safety in their neighbourhood. These individual responses tap the third dimension of 'grassing' identified here: the social.

Grassing and 'socialisation'

This third theme in the phenomenon of grassing returns us to the beliefs commented on above that, 'You're alright if you're local',. Other comments made to this effect were:

> I've lived here all my life and feel safe. What goes on here is a way of life. You have to stick up for yourself and teach kids to do the same. (Unemployed female, who had lived in the area for 40 years)

> It's safe for locals but not strangers in the area. (Middle aged male, unemployed, who had lived in the area for 29 years)

> Oldtown is a great area if you are a member of the community, went to the local school and grew up with the local villains, but terrible if you're an outsider. (Elderly female, who had lived in the area for 11 years)

> I've no real problems because I know the people and the area and grew up with local villains and know local youths. (Middle aged male, employed, who had lived in the area 35 years)

> If your face doesn't fit here you'll have problems, otherwise you're okay. (Housewife, who had lived in the area for 3 years)

All sorts of interesting questions are generated by this kind of assertion of locality. Despite the fact that according to the Home Office sponsored survey on witness intimidation, of the 35 people who had been a victim of crime in the previous year and recognised the offender, seven of those people knew the offender to be a neighbour on the estate; being local still seems to matter. When this belief about the importance of being local is put alongside people's other beliefs about crime discussed above the picture does become more complex.

The origins of these beliefs are probably not easy to identify, but the influence of the quasi-political network of the Salford Firm described above, is undoubtedly one key factor contributing to these responses. However it would appear that if you buy into the local dogma that 'criminals round here do not rob off their own', that you will be alright so long as you don't grass to the police or any other 'official', and that you accept the presence of alternative structures of control on the estate, then you can actually possess a sense of confidence, 'well-being' or ontological security in the ward of Oldtown.

It is important, however, not to overstate the prevalence or depth of this security. Residents also demonstrated that although they might accept that this code operates and appreciated the personal advantage it afforded them, they nevertheless worried about their children growing up in such an environment. Such concerns notwithstanding, the evidence that residents were aware of and in some sense believed in this code, regardless of whether or not it bore any actual relationship to empirical relaity, is significant in defining not only who belongs in the locality and who does not, but also in ensuring, at an individual level, a certain sense of security.

To summarise: whilst people living in this area were intimidated by the presence of the criminal gang and its activities, they also believed that that same presence afforded them a level of protection from criminal victimisation not provided by official agencies. Indeed, it was stated on more than one occasion by residents that they believed the presence of the Salford Firm had kept 'hard drugs' off the estate. Residents again and again emphasised the importance of being known locally and being known as local. One fourteen year old boy had this advice for people new to the area:

Make sure you know people.

The resultant effect of these findings seem to suggest that for people living in Oldtown, the notion of the 'fear of crime' is one that does not resonate with their expressed feelings about crime in their area. Their sense of belonging and the trust invested in the importance of being local, can equip people living in this area with a sense of security which is often not considered to be particularly problematic even though they may well have empirical evidence and experience of criminal activity which might suggest the contrary. Moreover this sense of security is shared by young and old, male and female alike. In some respects, then, these views leak an image of a highly organised community well defended from outsiders and outsiders' views of the area as problematic, in which the question of whom do you trust appears to be a salient one in understanding the management of 'ontological security' (Giddens, 1991).

Trust in Oldtown

As was sugggested in the previous chapter, the concept of trust has been relatively underexplored in the social sciences. The data presented in that chapter was clearly suggestive of the importance of understanding the mechanisms of trust and the way in which those mechanisms appeared to be mediated differently by age. In Oldtown it is clear that such mechanisms are also important but that they are also clearly mediated by different processes. Moreover, Fukuyama (1996), has argued that trust is also an essential part of modern life; that it is a requirement for creating 'regular, honest, behaviour'. Without such trust, Fukuyama suggests, economic relations cannot flourish. These relations, of course, are also relations which cannot be completely controlled; trust is therefore essential. The kinds of trust which exist, however, may not always be necessarily about creating 'regular honest behaviour' as Fukuyama states. Trust relationships may be just as likely be about creating regular dishonest behaviour. Arguably, it is the regularity or otherwise of the behaviour which sustains or threatens the trust relationship. The question for trust in Oldtown can be presented in the following way.

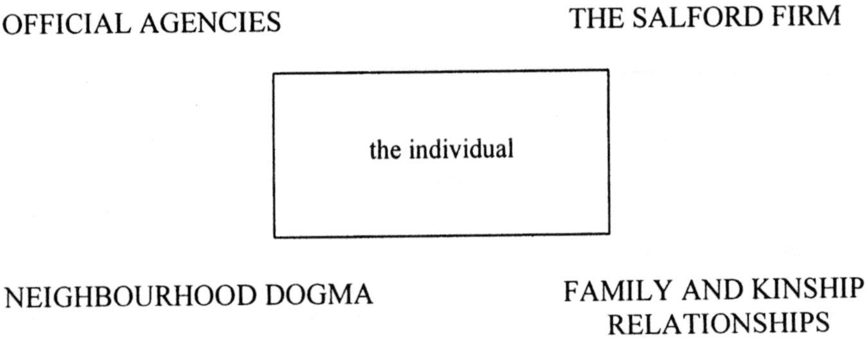

OFFICIAL AGENCIES   THE SALFORD FIRM

```
+----------------------------+
|                            |
|       the individual       |
|                            |
|                            |
+----------------------------+
```

NEIGHBOURHOOD DOGMA   FAMILY AND KINSHIP
                                        RELATIONSHIPS

Figure 3   The Square of Trust in Oldtown

In this square of trust, whom you can trust, how you trust, and how much you can trust (Nelken, 1994) at an individual levels depends upon where any individual finds themselves located in relation to these mechanisms. From the evidence discussed here it would appear that people trust as much as the local neighbourhood dogma permits whilst simultaneously endeavouring to avoid 'public shaming' (being labelled a 'grass'). This takes the form of, primarily, trusting other local people because they are local. This does not mean that other individuals are not to be trusted. But those other are trusted in a highly individualistic and fragile manner and the continuance of that trust is dependent upon what those individuals do with the trust invested in them. This may, for example, include trusting individual police officers and individual officials from other agencies, but it certainly does not mean offering generalised trust to those official agencies. The risks of public shaming are too high a price to pay for whatever benefits might accrue from engaging in such co-operation. It must be remembered, however, that the existence of these processes does not mean that the anarchistic politics of the criminal gang have won the hearts and minds of the people in this community. It just means that people seem to have found a way of managing their routine daily lives informed by the reality in which these lives are conducted. Moreover such mechanisms appear, for the most part, to cut across the barriers of age and gender.

Conclusion: Oldtown, a defended community?

From this discussion it is possible to argue that Oldtown, far from being the socially disorganised and disordered community that the sociological or the criminological literature might suggest, is a highly internally organised and ordered place. The nature of that organisation and order might challenge conventional conceptualisations of what might be considered to count as a more legitimate basis for community life, but this does not mean that such conventional understandings are absent from it (see the Conclusion for a fuller discussion of these particular implications). It does imply, however, that people living, working, and going to school in areas like Oldtown have found a way of creating an equilibrium between conventional expectations and their lived experiences.

For the people living in this area this equilibrium works most of the time. The local neighbourhood dogma equips them with a set of beliefs which enables sense to be made of their routine daily lives. This neighbourhood dogma also endorses the fierce sense of loyalty felt to this area by many people living within it; hence Oldtown may be best understood as a defended community. This defence, however, runs deeper than local neighbourhood dogma.   If trust, as a generative mechanism works in the way that has been suggested by the analysis offered here, then the roots of the defence to this community are deeply entrenched indeed.   Arguably this defence is historical in origin but hugely relevant in relation to contemporary practice.   Moreover understanding the nature of these trust relationships carries with it significant implications for not only understanding how it is that people feel safe here but also for what might impact or not impact upon these relationships in terms of crime prevention and policing (to be discussed in chapter four).

To summarise: the findings associated with Oldtown, whilst not predicted at the start of this research and certainly not predicted by the sociological and criminological literature of the United Kingdom, do resonate with some of the more ethnographic work of the United States (see for example, Merry, 1981; Anderson, 1990).   They are findings which undoubtedly pose a challenge to political and policy rhetoric about such areas alongside raising questions concerning the way in which the fear of crime has been so far understood and explored.   All of these issues will be returned to in the Conclusion.

Part Three: Crime, Policy and Community

4 Crime, Community and Partnership: Zero Tolerance or Community Tolerance?

Introduction

Three ideas have dominated the crime prevention debate during the 1990s; zero tolerance policing, partnership, and community. Each of these ideas have infiltrated policy and practice in different ways and each has a different genealogy. They have, however, become powerful rhetorical devices in political and policy discourse in informing and guiding practitioners along particular paths. Garland (1996) has argued that this process marks the culmination of a new way of governing the crime problem, that which he has labelled the responsibilization strategy.

> The recurring message of this approach is that the state alone is not, and cannot effectively be, responsible for preventing and controlling crime. Property owners, residents, retailers, manufacturers, town planners, school authorities, transport managers, employers, parents, and individual citizens - all of these must be made to recognise that they too have a responsibility in this regard, and must be persuaded to change their practices in order to reduce criminal opportunities and increase informal controls. In effect, central government is, in this field of policy as in several others, operating upon established boundaries which separate the private from the public realm, seeking to renegotiate the question of what is properly a state function and what is not (Garland, 1996: 453).

In the context of crime prevention this strategy is clearly associated with notions of 'partnership', 'multi-agency initiatives' and 'self-help' which Karmen (1990) In In the context of crime prevention this strategy is clearly associated with notions of 'partnership', 'multi-agency initiatives' and 'self-help' which Karmen (1990) has argued has demarcated a change of policy focus from crime prevention to victimisation prevention.   In the

101

context of policing it has been associated with the zero tolerance of anti-social behaviour; arguably re-establishing some of the more traditional foci of policework. These themes and their viability in high crime areas, underpin the focus of concern of this chapter.

Partnership and community

The notions of community and partnership have been linked in different ways since the early 1980s. Home Office circular 8/84 set in place the view that the responsibility for crime prevention was to be shared with the community. That circular emphasised multi-agency responses to crime prevention and sparked a number of government led initiatives from the Five Towns Initiative in 1986 to the launch of the Safer Cities Programme in 1988. During the 1980s considerable energy was put into schemes such as these. The kinds of specific policies put in place during this time varied from police-led Neighbourhood Watch schemes to (frequently) police-led multi-agency working. These top-down policy initiatives reflect, primarily, a territorial definition of community in which crime is seen as an external threat to it or, if seen as an internal problem, resulted in the further stereotyping of that community (Sampson et al., 1988).

It has to be said that the areas in which these kind of initiatives seem to have achieved most success have been the leafy suburbs not areas like Oldtown and Bankhill. The reasons for this may be manifold, but one key ingredient has to be the bias embedded in policy initiatives such as these towards areas in which some degree of social cohesion and community-agency co-operation already exists and, moreover, where rates of criminal victimisation may be relatively low. During the same decade NACRO endeavoured to enjoin the notions of partnership and community with a different emphasis; community safety. This emphasis adopts less a territorial understanding of community and more of a social one. It also proposes a co-operative approach to community crime prevention and endeavours to put in place mechanisms to ensure that community participation is both facilitated and representative. Endorsement was given to partnership as community safety in Home Office Circular 44/90, more often referred to as the Morgan Report, and appeared in the Home Secretary's Key Objectives for 1998-99. Arguably it is this view of partnership which received statutory endorsement in the Crime and Disorder Act 1998. The perceived relevance of zero tolerance policing to tackling the crime problem, arguably, has more complex origins.

Community and zero tolerance policing

The notion of Zero Tolerance as a campaigning slogan has its origins in North America. There is some dispute around who can claim ownership of the slogan itself but in the context of crime and criminal justice policy it is possible to trace two possible sources: feminist campaigns on violence against women and the 'broken windows' thesis of Wilson and Kelling (1982).

Feminist campaigns bearing the Zero Tolerance label arguably have their origins in Canada in the aftermath of the killing of fourteen female engineering students in Montreal in 1989. That event resulted in a strong public reaction to violence against women in general provoking the Family Violence Initiative on the part of the Canadian Government in its aftermath (Foley, 1993). The slogan of Zero Tolerance was imported from this initiative to Edinburgh in 1992 providing the impetus for a series of local authority led campaigns against violence against women and children.

This version of Zero Tolerance has a number of characteristics. It focuses on prevention, provision, and protection. Starting life as a phased poster campaign as a way of drawing public attention to violence against women and children, this is reinforced by paying detailed attention to the co-ordination of policies addressing women's and children's needs across and between different agencies, alongside a willingness to put some resources into ensuring that such policies are effective. Since 1992 a number of local authorities have initiated such campaigns.

The second way in which the notion of Zero Tolerance has been used by politicians and policy makers alike reflects a desire to gain public support for the so-called 'new look' policing policies which have gathered considerable momentum under this banner. In the U.K. from April to September 1997 there was a proliferation of seminars on Zero Tolerance aimed primarily at police officers. William J. Bratton, the doyen of Zero Tolerance in New York, headed one such seminar held at the Institute for Economic Affairs in July 1997 which launched the publication by him entitled *Zero Tolerance: Policing a Free Society.* Whilst Bratton does not claim to have read the by now (in)famous 'broken windows' essay by Wilson and Kelling, he does claim to have reached the same view of managing crime and crime related problems based on his own experience.

For Wilson and Kelling's 'broken windows' thesis a key indicator of social and environmental decline is the rise of incivilities. They express this in this way:

> A piece of property is abandoned, weeds grow up, a window is smashed. Adults stop scolding rowdy children; the children, emboldened, become more rowdy. Families move out, unmarried adults move in. Teenagers gather in front of the corner store. The merchant asks them to move, they refuse. Fights occur. Litter accumulates. (op. cit., 1982: 32)

A rise in these kinds of behaviours, they argue, make an area vulnerable to crime. In this way they construct an inextricable link between rising incivilities and rising crime. However, the empirical evidence to support this equation is ambivalent.

There does seem to be some relationship between the presence of incivilities and the fear of crime (Hope and Hough, 1988), on the other hand, however, there is some evidence to suggest that in areas undergoing gentrification (that is, urban incline), incivilities are also far from absent (Matthews, 1992: 31) and yet this does not seem to interfere with their economic growth and attractiveness. In other words, the evidence for the Wilson and Kelling equation is not clear.

In some respects the debate which has been generated by the 'broken windows' thesis reflects the fallacy referred to by Young (1997) as 'the social as simple'. It reflects a desire for the easy solution, the quick fix, to the complex ways in which social factors like the changing nature of the housing market, demography, the labour market, local road building policies, all have their different and differential impact on communities undergoing change. The quick fix in the 'broken windows' version of Zero Tolerance is aggressive policing.

Bratton (1997) argues that the policing problems facing New York at the beginning of the 1990s were epitomised by the failures inherent in the melding together of two different styles of policing: the three Rs (rapid response, random patrol, and reactive investigation) and the three Ps (partnership, problem solving, and prevention). In his view these two styles simply did not mix. The answer to these problems, and the proffered explanation for the decline in the New York crime rate, lay in three strategies:

1) the recruitment of more officers (seven thousand of them);
2) the offering of real empowerment within the police organisation at precinct level (characterised by a clear development of organisational goals, decentralisation, investing in computers, improvements in internal investigation, and regular meetings which call individuals to account);
3) the targeting of unacceptable public behaviour.

Bratton is vehemently committed to the view that this version of 'Zero Tolerance' worked in New York; it reduced crime. What many of those politicians and practitioners who have embraced this slogan seem to have obscured in their enthusiasm for it, is that there were three strands to the New York version of Zero Tolerance. One may not work without the others. Indeed arguably none of these strategies necessarily imply a zero tolerance of anything but more an acceptance that policing is a locally nuanced practice requiring the resources to solve local problems. There is nothing new in this as Pollard (1997), points out, and in the course of this chapter this is certainly a question to which we shall return. The question remains as to the relevance of these ideas of partnership and zero tolerance to Oldtown and Bankhill.

Crime, partnership and policing in Oldtown and Bankhill

As has been made clear elsewhere in this book, both of these areas are known as high crime areas. The locations are part of the Salford Division of the Greater Manchester Police. The recorded crime rate for Salford as a whole was, at the time of the study, significantly higher than the national average; for example, in 1992 the incidence of recorded crime in England and Wales was 10,500 offences per 100,000 population, in Salford it was 16,660. The two areas under investigation did not correspond with police boundaries, but the recorded burglary rate, for example, for the sub-division in which Bankhill was situated was 70.3 per 1000 population in 1993, and was 88.4 per 1000 population for the sub-division which included Oldtown. Moreover, police officers believed that there was a significant under-reporting of crime in each of these areas (see Evans and Walklate, 1997). Indeed, our own criminal victimisation survey conducted in August 1994 reported that 23.7% of people in Oldtown and 36.9% of people in Bankhill were victims of crime in the previous year. Analysis of Command and Control data covering the beats relevant to these two localities for the month of January 1995 indicated that on a daily average 21 incidents were reported in Oldtown (1 per 11 residents) and 24 in Bankhill (1 per 24 residents); though, of course, it must be remembered that not all of these incidents (calls for service) are necessarily crime related nor are they necessarily recorded as crimes. A more detailed analysis of that Command and Control data suggests that these two wards report a different pattern of incidents.

Table 1 Incidents by Ward (Command and Control Data, January 1995)

TYPE OF INCIDENT	OLDTOWN	BANKHILL
Vehicle crime	33%	24%
Property crime	15%	26%
Personal crime	8%	14%
Nuisance/suspicion	12%	9%
Child at risk/abuse	<1%	2%
Road traffic accident	1%	2%
Drugs/drink related	<1%	<1%
Activated alarms	20%	9%
Non-crime related	9%	14%
Total number of incidents	649	737

On their own, these data offer a superficial insight into the nature of *reported local* (crime) problems. What they reveal is the level and kind of demand made on local policing resources as initiated by members of the public. Consequently they reflect the kind and type of incidents which those same members of the public are comfortable with defining as appropriate for police action.   Taking such factors into account, this distribution is particularly interesting in (at least) two respects. First in respect of the differential proportion of reported incidents in each area relating to vehicle and property crime. Second, in respect of the proportion of reported incidents relating to drugs/ drink. Each of these concerns are differentially reflected in other sources of data gathered during the course of this project.

Part of the data gathering process involved the application of a fairly conventional criminal victimisation survey (596 completed questionnaires in total: 300 in Bankhill, 296 in Oldtown). Responses to those survey questions offer another insight into individual members of the community's concerns about crime. Respondents in both area were asked which issues, from a list, they thought were either a problem or a big problem in their areas. Responses in the following table are ordered according to the frequency with which they were cited as either a problem or a big problem in their area.

Table 2 Issues Considered to be a Problem or a Big Problem in Their Area

PROBLEM/BIG PROBLEM	OLDTOWN	BANKHILL
Vandalism	187	228
Crime	162	224
Young people hanging about	152	190
Unemployment	151	166
No play area	141	160
Graffiti	107	126

(Numbers listed reflect total number of mentions by respondents in each area in order of frequency mentioned.)

This kind of listing is indicative of the degree of consensus which exists between people living in these areas in relation to what they considered to be local problems. The ordering of these problems changes somewhat when respondents were asked what was a particular problem for *them* in *their* area. For people in Bankhill crime still topped the list with vandalism coming second; for people in Oldtown this concern was superseded by having nowhere for their children to play with crime coming second. So the ordering of local problems changes; but crime still features as an issue affecting people. This was reiterated by the evidence of the kinds of crime people worried about happening to them during the day and during the night in their areas.

Table 3   Crimes Worried About During the Day and During the Night in Each Area

CRIME WORRY	DAYTIME		NIGHT-TIME	
	OLDTOWN	BANKHILL	OLDTOWN	BANKHILL
Being burgled	131(1st)	173(1st)	130(1st)	168(1st)
Car being stolen	80(2nd)	80(3rd)	78(2nd)	82(5th)
Vandalism	65(3rd)	92(2nd)	57(6th)	89(4th)
Being robbed	40(4th)	65(4th)	50(8th)	76(6th)
Young people	39(5th)	45(5th)	57(6th)	69(7th)
Being attacked	30(6th)	44(6th)	51(7th)	60(8th)
Being out alone	29(7th)	43(7th)	74(3rd)	108(2nd)

(Numbers reflect relative frequency of mentions by respondents with relative ranking in brackets.)

Whilst there is little of surprise here given the more general findings of the criminal victimisation survey industry, these figures do endorse the extent to which people living in each of these localities shared common concerns about crime and the crime problem. Although, of course, the variable frequency with which some crimes were mentioned may reflect different levels of concern. For example, those respondents in Oldtown who reported having been a victim of crime in the previous year (69 in total) reported 20 burglaries, 2 robberies, 31 thefts, and 27 incidents of criminal damage; those respondents in Bankhill who reported having been a victim of crime in the previous year (111 in total) reported 53 burglaries, 5 robberies, 35 thefts, and 38 incidents of criminal damage. These expressed concerns reinforce the reporting pattern indicated by the Command and Control data.

Sources of data such as these provide one way of constructing an understanding of the crime problem in each of these localities; and, consequently, one way of formulating policy responses to that problem. Indeed, the policy implementation process suggested by the Morgan Report (1990) recommends that such sources of data are used in order to inform community safety initiatives. Using data sources such as these, it could be taken that the crime problem in these two localities is of a fairly conventional nature, that is, burglary, car crime and criminal damage. Consequently practitioners may be persuaded that policy could also be conventionally informed; for example, the introduction and resourcing of Neighbourhood Watch Schemes as a means of tackling burglary. However reliance on such data sources alone would address only the surface manifestation of the crime problem in localities such as Oldtown and Bankhill. These data do not penetrate its deep structure. Other sources of information provide an insight into this. One place in which clues to this deep structure can be found is in the discussions which took place in the local Police Community Consultative Forums in each of these areas during the research period.

Police Community Consultative Group meetings, held monthly, were attended regularly by around thirty people from Oldtown and towards sixty in the Bankhill area. Analysis of the minutes of these meetings from February 1994 to July 1996 revealed that there were four recurring themes to those meetings in both areas; how to deal with troublesome youth, the problem of intimidation, the impact of force restructuring, and the slow response to 999 calls. In addition in Bankhill frequent concern was expressed about the possible closure of the local police station and the rapidity of turnover of local police personnel. So whilst what went on in police community consultative meetings does not match exactly the concerns highlighted from our survey data, there was enough similarity in the concerns expressed to suggest that such meetings were not just giving a voice to those who chose to attend, but were tapping more widely held community concerns. What is particularly interesting in respect of those more widely held community concerns is the expressed problem of intimidation. In-depth interview and focus group data gathered in both of these areas facilitated a deeper understanding of what this more qualitative talk about crime articulates.

Talk about crime in Oldtown

Depending upon where you live in Oldtown the experience of crime can be very different. In the Canalside and The Way parts of the ward (where the incidence of home ownership is at its highest), people were concerned that their houses or sheds might be broken into or objects taken from their garden. In discussion groups in these areas, as we discussed earlier, we found that people were much more likely to talk about taking preventive measures against crime- planting prickly shrubs near fences or buying alarms for houses and cars. Crime here was talked about as a nuisance rather than a major threat to peace of mind. However in other parts of the ward, particularly The Triangle, the central talk about crime focused on groups of young males who gathered in particular parts of the estate and were seen to be involved in a good deal of anti-social behaviour. It is here that we can begin to get a feel for the problem of intimidation.

The problem of intimidation has been discussed in the context of Oldtown in greater detail elsewhere (see chapter three and Evans, Fraser, and Walklate, 1996). Indeed, in 1994 the area was chosen as part of a Home Office sponsored survey dealing with the question of intimidation but the survey was left incomplete as the interviewers were 'asked' to leave the area after two days! As chapter three also demonstrated the idea that 'you're alright round here if you're local' has considerable force; and 'being local' has less to do with length of residence than sticking to a particular code of conduct. This code includes not 'grassing to the police' and not openly working against the interests of the criminal gang. In return the gang offers to cut down on the number of local people who will be victims of crime by letting people know that crime against local people will not be tolerated and by punishing those who break this code.

The gang therefore can and does intimidate local residents; many of whom keep quiet and do not 'grass' to the authorities rather than incur the displeasure of the gang. Indeed, the public shaming area discussed in chapter threee, in the middle of Oldtown, used to daub names of 'grasses' on prominent walls, acts as a very public reminder of the alternative structures of control on the estate. Moreover, even those residents who called the police, reported feeling undermined by the length of time it could take for the police to respond which further marginalised them and fostered a reliance on the view that local people are better relied on to sort things out (see Evans and Walklate, 1996). The underlying mechanisms which support these processes have been discussed elsewhere in relation to the question of trust (see chapters two and three, and Walklate, 1998).

Talk about crime in Bankhill

To recap, walking around Bankhill the pedestrian can encounter areas which differ in their appearance and their 'feel'. Some areas look well-cared for and largely clear of rubbish and vandalism; whereas others are heavily painted with graffiti and may have other signs of disorder such as large numbers of boarded up windows, rubbish strewn back alleys and houses with windows which are shuttered and /or barred. Such places might amount to 'hotspots' for crime; and indeed in discussion groups a number of people said that they found it easier to cope with burglary than with the petty crime engendered by such locations. For example, if the grids and drain covers along their street were stolen people must wait for the appropriate agency to act; if empty houses were vandalised then it would be up to others to initiate repairs. But such signs of disorder also signalled a more general deterioration and loss of faith in their neighbourhood. The view was frequently expressed that, 'this area is going downhill rapidly'. This view, alongside the construction of young people as 'people to be feared' had an enormous impact in Bankhill.

As the survey data cited above for Bankhill indicated, a substantial percentage of people living in this ward worried about young people hanging around on the streets. Indeed in many parts of the ward groups of young people, primarily male but not solely, were very visible, and whilst a proportion of these young people would have been involved in criminal activity, such activity was (at the time of this study) not as well organised as in Oldtown. As a consequence, local residents appeared to see all young people as people to be feared, avoided, and mistrusted. As one middle aged woman stated:

We've reached the stage where we suspect children, all children, and youths and girls. You suspect them all.

Such views have an enormous impact on old and young in this neighbourhood. They have not as yet, however, undermined the willingness of people living in this area to work with the official agencies to try to improve matters and to look to such agencies for guidance and solutions. (The dynamics underpinning Bankhill have been discussed more fully in chapter two).

To summarise: for Oldtown, people feel they know who the criminals are, and feel that they know who will solve local 'disputes'. They also know something about the highly organised nature of crime in their area. Based on this knowledge they know who to trust, who not to trust, when and how. Police officers managing and working in this area also know some of these things. They also know that they are, for the most part, marginal to these processes unless the equilibrium between them, the community, and the criminals becomes unbalanced in some way. In these circumstances Oldtown becomes a policing problem for both the police and the residents alike. They both 'know' that targeting troublesome youth, in and of itself, would not begin to penetrate the organised nature of crime in this area. (These issues are discussed more fully below).

For Bankhill, people also know who the criminals are: 'young people'. What they do not know is who is going to sort out their local 'disputes'. What they do know is that they would like the 'officials' to do something, whilst at the same time they lack the belief and level of sociability to know how or what to do for themselves. Crime in this area is prevalent, but relatively disorganised, and people know who they want to trust (the officials) and who they distrust (young people). However, because of the relative disorganisation of criminality and community relationships in this area, this knowledge remains fragile. Such fragility, alongside the belief that 'This area is going downhill rapidly' means that there is little for people to rely on in terms of community and/or social infrastructure. Targeting the troublesome behaviour of young people in this area, which a simple aggressive policing style like Zero Tolerance might do, *might* have an effect on the local fear of crime (Hope and Hough, 1988) but would not solve the other problems for people in this area (for example, unemployment, neglect of properties, absence of community relationships, poor health etc).

Putting all these observations together, this data is clearly suggestive of the need for a finely nuanced policy response based on an understanding of the specific difficulties faced by *both* the agencies working within an area *and* the potentially variable community dynamics of that area. To reiterate; the areas under discussion here were less than two miles apart, yet the question of what might work in each of them looks potentially very different. That question of what might work is rooted in the lived reality of the crime problem in these areas and how the people living there respond to it.   So what implications might findings such as these have for the question of generating community partnerships in this area?

Crime, partnership, and community safety

As was stated at the beginning of this chapter 'partnership' has become the new buzzword of the crime prevention industry. Indeed there is an argument that it is no bad thing that the responsibility for the 'crime problem' is owned by an increasingly diffuse variety of individuals and organisations. There is a point of view, for example, which would render rational the demand from insurance companies that people living in certain post code areas must fit particular types of door and window locks before becoming eligible for household insurance. On the other hand some of the dangers inherent in this diffusion of responsibility, especially at an organisational level, have been alluded to by Crawford (1997). He situates the appeals to 'community' and 'partnership' as part of the wider process of the governance (as opposed to government) of crime; that is, as part of the increasingly shifting and opaque boundaries between the state and other intraorganisational networks (the public, the private, the voluntary sector) who have become ever more involved in managing the crime problem. He discusses the opportunity for such intraorganisational networks to become increasingly influential, for example, in relation to what kind of crime prevention initiative might be funded, how that might be managed etc. and yet at the same time lack accountability (Crawford, 1994).

    Analyses of the strengths and weaknesses of the partnership approach such as that offered by Crawford are more than viable if researchers and policy makers alike insist on looking for solutions to the crime problem from the top down. What about looking from the bottom up? (Lewis and Salem, 1986). Can community safety partnerships prevent, reduce, or manage crime in areas like Oldtown and Bankhill? If so what kind of crime, how and under what circumstances, with what kind of partnerships?

    For example, at the time the research was conducted in Bankhill there was a great willingness on the part of the community to work for change. Such willingness was expressed in both the desire to work with the 'authorities' and the trust invested in them to be able to make things happen. In return, people in Bankhill wanted their concerns, which may appear petty and trivial (criminal damage and vandalism), to be taken seriously by the 'authorities'. Consequently, in an area like this, the local authority and the police may be able to take a lead in local developments and will find support for such in the local community. Support which may be best harnessed by exploring interpretations of the notion of partnership above and beyond the more normatively prescribed multi-agency approach.

This kind of strategy implies the view that crime is a local problem to be *managed* locally, not necessarily prevented or reduced. So the result may not be crime prevention or even crime reduction, but management; that is, ensuring that people feel better about, and more in control of, what is going on in their area. By implication this vision of the relationship between partnership and crime embraces the importance of managing incivilities as highlighted by the 'broken windows' thesis of Wilson and Kelling; 1982, but with perhaps a rather different focus on who is responsible for that process.

The construction of young people as 'people to be feared' in Bankhill might demand a different response again. On a longer term basis this is, arguably, the most pressing problem in this area. At present Bankhill offers little to young people and they in return are hesitant to go out of 'their area' to use what facilities there are. This may well be the space in which partnerships between teachers, youth workers, private enterprise, parents and the young people themselves (and other relevant agencies) might work most effectively.

On the other hand, in Oldtown the crime problem is already being managed, not by a community safety partnership strategy, but through the (fragile) equilibrium between the police, the local community, and the organised nature of crime in that area. A very different conception of what might constitute a partnership! Yet, the processes underpinning these relationships, in allowing people to feel alright about living in their locality, seems to work for most of the people living there most of the time. Of course, relationships such as these make agency-led interventions a difficult prospect in areas like Oldtown. Moreover in different localities in this ward, very local problems have been managed by local residents working together, sometimes with official aid coming afterwards, sometimes with that aid not being forthcoming at all.

In other words, partnerships in areas like Oldtown might well be formed but they may not have any of the characteristics of conventional organisational (voluntary or otherwise) allegiances; such partnerships may be with strategically placed individual residents, for example. Again, understanding the problem to be managed may be primarily about that, management. The desired result may not be crime prevention or crime reduction but the restoration of local equilibrium; that is a way of managing the differences and similarities within in local community. The question of establishing a working equilibrium in communities returns us to the question of policing and the relevance of the zero tolerance approach.

Policing, crime and community in Oldtown and Bankhill

This discussion draws both implicitly and explicitly on a number of different sources of police related data; walking the areas with police officers, in-depth interviews with relevant senior personnel, and focus group discussions held with Inspectors and Community Beat Officers. It should be noted that the researchers felt that the police officers who participated in this study were as frank and as open as it was possible for them to be given the nature of their work and of this particular study. It should also be noted that all the officers who participated in this part of the study were male. What will be explored here is the similarities and differences between police managers and beat officers and between police talk and community talk about crime in these two areas.

In discussion the police managers, whilst in agreement as to what constituted the main crime problem in these localities (the level of (dis)organised crime amongst youths) also recognised them as areas with different policing needs. For example, one police inspector said:

> I think there's a subtle difference. I think that the number of villains that live in Oldtown and live in Bankhill, per house population, is probably very similar. The Oldtown villains don't tend to commit as much crime in Oldtown as the Bankhill criminals (do in Bankhill). Oldtown seems to export a lot of their problems. I'm not saying that that doesn't happen in Bankhill. I don't think it happens to the same extent ..... yes I know that it's (Oldtown is) a tough old place.... but I don't perceive that the residents are in the same sort of position as they are in Bankhill.

Several reasons were offered for these differences between Oldtown and Bankhill by these police managers:

> In Oldtown there are seen to be no victims - just insurance companies that bear the brunt of crime.

> Residents don't see the victims, the victims are not living locally .... so there's no sort of bond, whether it be a good or a bad bond.

> Residents are more likely to hold to the view that - it's OK because all the victims are rich anyway.

So in some respects these police managers' views of Oldtown as a defended community mirror what the residents told us; the idea that 'people round here don't rob off their own'. There is a danger here, of course, that what has been tapped is a self fulfilling prophecy, especially given the historical reputation of this particular area; though the data presented here does not have the capacity to explore the extent to which this is or is not the case. Moreover the project was not established to engage in that kind of work. What is more important, perhaps, in relation to policy possibilities, is to understand the potential impact of such views. In this respect it will be of value to explore these initial images in more detail.

Policing Oldtown

The views of the police managers went on to endorse the multifaceted nature of Oldtown as a defended community. As one of the inspectors stated:

> We've got the residents on Canalside, we've got businesses on Broadway and we've got Oldtown itself. There's lots of separate communities there. When I'm thinking about community policing, I never think of that line there (on the map) as a community with the same problems.

The existence of different communities within this ward was also recognised by the residents, who told us on more than one occasion of their belief that different parts of the areas were policed differently. This concern was expressed in two ways; police response to 999 calls (a constant feature of Police Community Consultation Group meetings referred to above), and concern about the allocation of resources. In both cases the belief was expressed by residents on more than one occasion that the more recently developed business and residential part of the ward (especially Canalside) was in receipt of preferential treatment. Indeed analysis of command and control data endorses residents' experience insofar as those parts of the ward in which most businesses are situated made more 999 calls to the police; calls which received a higher priority response because they were from businesses than 999 calls from other parts of the ward. When this possibility was put to this group of police managers, the following responses were elicited.

> It's the other way round, sorry very much the other way round. The estate is potentially a major problem. But you've also got to be careful not to put too many resources there, and they're likely to kick off, not that it's a no-go, but you don't want to make problems for yourself.

And:

> You've got the actual Oldtown housing estate itself, and two area officers, and all the rest on this map has got one. That's the measure of it. Certainly in terms of patrols, the section patrols, they cover the whole area, they're not allocated to one particular area. I can probably understand their (the residents) concerns, because Canalside, for example, have funded their own private security control.

facing police officers and managers in the 'estate' in Oldtown. The comment was made that the estate was very 'resource intensive; you have to have two officers going out to any incident - one who guards the car'. There was a good deal of strong feeling and disagreement about what might work in this area but there was a consensus concerning the difficulty of getting any intelligence information from the residents on the estate because:

> The police are marginalised, a resident will only talk to the police if the resident feels that they will get something out of the conversation.

And:

> It's very difficult. It's easy when you just have victims but when you've got a mixture of both victims and villains, it's not quite so simple.

And:

> You're fighting a losing battle ... you can try everything but you can only get into people's minds, take them individually and try to reprogram them to what's right and wrong.

For these police managers, then, the unwillingness of this defended community to 'grass' (those living on the estate in particular), to talk to any official, least of all the police, is a central issue in the management of the crime problem. These officers, reflected in their comments, the need for intelligence in order to render the police less marginal to the residents of the estate in particular and the area in general.

This issue of marginality was, however, felt most acutely by the officers on the beat. They talked of feeling totally excluded from the estate and described the community and its residents in the following terms; 'a clan', 'it's close-knit'. They felt of little use and told us that; 'After a crime, they're looking after themselves'; and from a police point of view, 'It's impossible to police'. All of these feelings are encapsulated in the following statement:

> It's always been a self-policing community ..... they still dislike vandalism, and they dislike most crime that goes on, but they are unwilling to break from the community chapel. The community is strangling itself.

In many ways these beat officers feel that they have 'lost' this area because; 'kids are seeing that crime pays in this area'; 'they are using criminals as role models'; and they recognise that local people are forced to accommodate what happens around them; 'they've a high threshold' in accepting levels of crime.

Their solutions to the policing problems of the estate lie not so much in the need for effective intelligence but in talk of 'taking out' fifteen to twenty families from the estate and removing fifty to sixty lads. This, they argued, would leave the rest of the community free from intimidation and remove the example of the successful criminal life.

Policing Bankhill

The key policing problem in Bankhill, as defined by the police managers, is youths on the street. As one Inspector stated:

> People would say they're just kids on bikes, but it is actually really organised crime. That's a big issue in this area. It's very primitive in respect of signals by whistling, so on and so forth, but nonetheless it goes on, and the residents are aware that it goes on, and they're very, very, fearful of it.

The officers then went on to discuss the level of intimidation they believed to exist in this area and argued that this resulted in an unrealistically low officially recorded crime rate. Because of the level of fear and intimidation in the area there was also a recognition and acceptance of the view that what the community wanted was high profile policing. Moreover, because of the unrealistic officially recorded crime rate resulting from the levels of intimidation, these managers struggled to justify the allocation of more resources to the area; yet intermittently tried to put this in place anyway. Their talk was of marrying high profile policing with covert surveillance as a way of managing the crime problem in this locality. Indeed, whilst they again acknowledged that this was very resource intensive, they felt that in circumstances where the community was too afraid to act upon its own knowledge of events in the area it was the role of the police to collate such knowledge.

This group of Inspectors demonstrated a good deal of knowledge about local people and their experiences of living in this area. They recognised that, whilst there was still a significant amount of community willingness to talk to the police this was consistently undermined by the distorted nature of everyday relationships within the area. So they told us:

> The people in this area have no trust, even of their own sons.

So they knew they were asking a great deal of local people in asking for their trust. They talked of a certain amount of trust existing between members of the public and individual police officers:

> Community policemen, they are known by people on their patch, and they will happily go and say I'll talk to Jim or Mark or whoever the police officer is, and they will tell him what's going on.

But these police managers also knew that the people in this community felt let down by the system in three ways; by regional police management who do not see a street robbery or an assault as something that is important in the sense that they fail to understand the extent to which the sheer weight of occurrence of robberies serves to keep people fearful and withdrawn from each other; by the court system which is not in tune with frightened communities in the sentences that it metes out; by local police management insofar as it has changed four times in two years with there being no Superintendent at the local station at one point during the research. Taken together these factors, they felt, affected the level of trust between the local police and the community giving the appearance of a lack of commitment to the area on the part of the police.

Overall the police management talk in relation to Bankhill, the frightened community, reflects a sense of impotence not as a result of the marginalisation of the police but from the fact that the residents in this community are actually looking to the police to solve all the area's problems. As was suggested by the data cited earlier; people in Bankhill see crime as their number one problem; solve the crime problem and everything else will fall back into place. Moreover these police officers said:

> I think we would be naive in the extreme to think that we, the police, can solve the problems in an area like Bankhill.

and went on to talk about the value of partnership working in this community as well as looking for ways of encouraging both individuals and local groups to 'stand up and be counted'.

This notion of 'Stand up and be counted' caused the beat officers in this area considerable difficulty. They were as aware as their management that to ask someone to take a stand is to expose them to levels of victimisation that can be unbearable. As one officer said it is easy to see what might be done in the abstract but much harder to put that into practice.

> People say, should I report it?, I've got two hats on then. I've got my civilian hat and my police hat. My police hat says, yes you must report this crime, that's the right thing to do, that's what society demands of us, stand up against these people. My other hat, my heart says, listen don't report it, because you're going to get your windows put in, you'll get your tyres slashed, you're going to get your car wrecked, you're going to get your daughter slapped, your son punched... Put it down to experience and hope it will go away....

These officers talked of the extreme stress they felt at working under these circumstances, of being 'worn down' and 'fatigued'. Moreover they too felt somewhat abandoned by their own organisation (given the impact of re-organisation) and looked for some sense of direction from within the force as to how to manage the day to day issues in this area. Their own solutions ranged from improving public education with respect to crime prevention to dealing with landlords who fail to look after property to the lack of father figures in single parent households. In a heated discussion on these issues came the following outburst:

> It's the adage, you live by the sword, you die by the sword. That's the way these people live. They are so violent, they are so ruthless, no scruples. It's

an old myth that honour among thieves. It's grass on the other before he grasses on you.

Such a response, and the wide ranging nature of 'the solutions' suggested by these officers reflects not only their deep concern for the area in which they were working but also their deep sense of frustration concerning what it was they could actually do. In some respects this frustration also constituted a conduit for their own frustration with the police organisation which they felt alienated from. They too, like the residents who attended the police community consultative groups for this area, expressed concern about the frequency of changes in management and the routine absence of a senior officer in their local station.

To summarise: on the one hand, it is possible to sense a degree of consensus between the police managers and the beat officers in their talk about Oldtown, a talk that up to a point mirrored that of the community. That consensus reflected a concern to manage the crime problem in Oldtown 'sensitively', partly because of the nature of criminality in that area and partly because lack of intelligence gave them few other options. Indeed, so long as there was a continued equilibrium between the marginality of the police and the self-policing nature of the community, Oldtown posed few serious problems. This equilibrium means that each have a way of managing the areas problems: the police can blame the residents and the residents can blame the police.

On the other hand, such a consensus is much more difficult to glean from the policetalk in Bankhill. Arguably, this lack of consensus is as much a consequence of the (felt) physical abandonment of lower ranking officers in Bankhill as it is a reflection of a lack of understanding of the policing needs in this area. Indeed, in some respects, it is possible to identify a degree of unity on this issue between the beat officers and the residents, but this unity is fragile because of the deeply felt frustrations of the beat officers. The fragility of these internal police relationships almost mirror the fragility of the social relationships found in Bankhill itself. Identified earlier as a 'frightened community', largely because of the rapidity of social change and the nature of criminality in the area, it is easy to see how lower ranking officers, who had also undergone a period of rapid organisational change, might feel uncertain as to their role not only in the community but also in the organisation. Residents in Bankhill do want to work with the police, do trust them, and look to them. This too unsettles the beat officers because they know that following the policing line may not actually help the residents. So what might work?

Policing, crime and community: zero tolerance or community tolerance?

Superficially, it is easy to see how the notion of Zero Tolerance might fit the two areas under discussion here. As research areas they could easily be mistaken for those kind of areas discussed by Wilson and Kelling (1982). Moreover, the criminal victimisation survey data gathered for this study and cited earlier indicates that vandalism, graffiti, troublesome youth, and crime were considered to be a big problem in both areas and some of these were also echoed in the policetalk about these areas. These are exactly those behaviours which have been targeted by Zero Tolerance policing. However, to adopt a Zero Tolerance stance unthinkingly in the areas under discussion here would miss the mark in both understanding the nature of the problems being faced in each of these communities and the nature of the problems facing the police officers. It will be useful to clarify further the implications of this statement.

To reiterate; Oldtown and Bankhill present themselves on the surface as facing very similar socio-economic circumstances. Indeed a superficial reading of the official crime figures and the criminal victimisation survey data presented here would suggest a similar conclusion with respect to crime. Such a reading would, however, gloss some of the important differences between these two communities in their management of their local crime problem. An effort has been made to capture these differences by talking of one as a 'defended' community and the other as a 'frightened' community. Each of these labels conveys different messages concerning what is it that people know, and what it is that needs to be known, about the crime problem in each of these localities; some of which is tapped by police officers.

As has been stated earlier, in Oldtown people know who the criminals are, and they know who will solve local 'disputes', they also know something about the highly organised nature of crime in their area. As a consequence of this knowledge they know who to trust, who not to trust, when and how. Police officers managing and working in this area also know some of these things and also know that they are, for the most part, marginal to these processes unless the equilibrium between them, the community, and the criminals becomes unbalanced in some way. In these circumstances Oldtown becomes a policing problem for both the police and the residents alike. They both 'know' that targeting troublesome youth, in and of itself, would not begin to penetrate the organised nature of crime in this area. This does not make this community any less moral, or have any less of a moral voice (Etzioni, 1997), as hopefully some of the data here has indicated, but it does provide this community with a way of managing everyday life. Moreover, as a result of this knowledge the police managers are correct in their view that in order to change the relationship between the police, the criminals, and the community, requires intelligence. Intelligence they are unlikely to receive unless the balance of relationships within this community radically alters in some way. Zero Tolerance policing, either in its simple aggressive form or in the version presented by Bratton, does not talk in these terms.

For Bankhill, people also know who the criminals are: 'young people'. What they do not know is who is going to sort out their local 'disputes', but what they do know is that they would like the 'officials' to do something. Crime in this area is prevalent, but relatively disorganised, and people know who they want to trust ('the officials') and who they distrust (young people). However, because of the relative disorganisation of criminality in this area, this knowledge is uncertain. That uncertainty, alongside the belief that 'This area is going downhill rapidly' means that there is little for people to rely on despite their willingness to do so. The community officers also reflect such uncertainty in their relationship with the police organisation in general and, as a consequence, also seem uncertain as to what they should do. Again simply targeting the troublesome behaviour of young people in this area, which a simple aggressive policing style might do, might have an effect on the fear of crime (Hope and Hough, 1988) but would not solve the other problems in this area; the changing nature of community relationships on the one hand and the difficulties being faced by police officers on the other. Bratton's threefold approach might be more effective, especially in its efforts to address the question of internal police organisation especially if it were combined with initiating and developing partnerships within the locality.

Conclusion

Sennett states:

> One of the unintended consequences of modern capitalism is that it has strengthened the value of place, aroused a longing for community. All the emotional conditions we have explored in the workplace animate that desire: the uncertainties of flexibility; the absence of deeply rooted trust and commitment; the superficiality of teamwork; most of all the specter of

failing to make something of oneself in the world, to 'get a life' through one's work. All of these conditions impel people to look for some other scene of attachment and depth. (1998:138)

Here Sennett is referring to the processes which underpin the emergence of what he calls the 'dangerous pronoun': we. Some of those dangers have been alluded to in the discussion here.

In moving towards the responsibilization strategy within the criminal justice arena as identified by Garland (1996), the presence and impact of the 'we' pronoun has certainly been felt. What this discussion has demonstrated, hopefully, is that the 'we' needs to be problematised; whose 'we', where, when, how? Who is to say that such a 'we' is present or absent? What and who might constitute the best sources of knowledge in answering such questions? Whose 'we' defines what is and is not to be tolerated and by whom? All questions which the data presented here stand as testimony to, at a minimum, the need for finely nuanced policy responses based on an understanding of the specific difficulties faced by both the agencies working within an area and the variable community dynamics of an area.

Of course, Sennett's analysis of this 'dangerous pronoun' is as concerned with the impact of the changing nature of capitalism and the impact of those changes on the nature of work on us all, as he might be concerned with the more specific implications of such processes on the policy possibilities for such communities like Oldtown and Bankhill. However the changing nature of capitalism has had its impact on communities like these too; most keenly felt in the presence and/or absence of work, and the uncertainties associated with that as with the increasingly flexible nature of work. This impact, arguably renders the notion of the presumptions which might underpin the 'dangerous pronoun' all the more poignant. Some of these issues are more fully explored in our conclusion.

Conclusion: Understanding and Managing Crime in High Crime Areas

Introduction

Communities, like the ones that have been the focus of concern of this book, are not unusual. Arguably, such communities have been the centre of different political and policy concern since the emergence of those parts of the city which have become known as the 'inner city'. In the United Kingdom's more recent history, marked as it has been by the inner city disturbances of 1981 and 1991, the problematic status assigned to such areas has become more acute. That problematic status is embedded in a number of presumptions about the nature of life in the inner city, about the norms and values to be associated with people who live in such areas, and about the most appropriate way of understanding the connections between crime and the fear of crime in such areas. The political and policy challenge presented by such areas is aptly illustrated in the opening statement of the Social Exclusion Unit Report 'Bringing Britain together: a national strategy for neighbourhood renewal' (1998):

> Over the last generation, this has become a more divided country. While most areas have benefited from rising living standards, the poorest neighbourhoods have tended to become more rundown, more prone to crime, and more cut off from the labour market. The national picture conceals pockets of intense deprivation where the problems of unemployment and crime are acute and hopelessly tangled up with poor health, housing, and education. They have become no go areas for some and no exit zones for others. In England as a whole the evidence we have suggests there are several thousand neighbourhoods and estates whose condition is critical, or soon could be.

However, the question of what may or may not work to improve the social and economic conditions in such areas is highly dependent upon what kind of assumptions have been made about the nature of such localities in the first instance. Drawing on the empirical findings of this study,   we shall explore some of those assumptions along three dimensions: understanding the first instance. Drawing on the empirical findings of this study, we shall explore some of those assumptions along three dimensions: understanding the inner city, understanding the fear of crime debate, and understanding the question of policy.

Understanding the inner city

As was suggested in the Introduction to this book, presumptions concerning the lived reality of the inner city abound in academic, political, and policy discourses. The origins of those presumptions are to be found in the political and policy drive to assert some control over the impact of the industrial revolution and the concomitant growth in urban development.   Added to these processes was the Chicago School's concern with understanding and managing the social disorganisation which became associated with the zone of transition (see the Introduction). The image of the inner city as socially disorganised has remained, and some would say has been perpetuated in more recent years in the United Kingdom, through the importation of the underclass debate and the ideas of comunitarianism from North America. Each of these debates have had their different impact upon images of inner city communities.

On the one hand, the underclass debate presumes that those people living in the inner city [inter alia] are cynical towards the official societal values (especially with respect to issues of law and order); have distinctive norms and values; and that they do not possess the capacity for conventional collective political action. (See for example, Murray, 1990). Consequently inner city communities, and the social problems they represent, are seen to constitute a threat to mainstream society. On the other hand, the communitarians, as articulated in the ideas of Etzioni (1996), argue for the need to restore communities with a new sense of moral, social, and public order reflecting a view that such processes are absent from existing community life.   In the light of the empirical evidence we have presented in this book we would argue that each of these views are flawed in different ways.

One key message from the empirical investigation under discussion here is the central difficulty of assuming all inner city areas are the same. The two areas under investigation were less than two miles apart, yet displayed very different ways of managing their relationship with crime. One, Oldtown, it is possible to argue, is a well organised, socially ordered, indeed well defended community, whose mechanisms of social control co-exist with more conventional processes. In this community people, for the most part, worked with the local neighbourhood dogma. It equipped them, not only with a sense of well-being, but also with a sense of moral, social, and public order, and simultaneously did not appear to undermine their capability for both conventional and unconventional collective action. The other, Bankhill, it is possible to argue, was a relatively disorganised, disordered, frightened community with a shifting sense of moral, social, and public order which did appear to undermine the capacity for any kind of collective action (conventional or otherwise) yet at the same time this did not seem to undermine the acceptance of official norms and values. It is worth reviewing each of these assertions about these two areas in greater detail.

One of the presumptions embedded within the debate around inner city areas is that the people who live in such areas have a cynical view of official societal values. Cynicism towards official societal values may be illustrated by expressed attitudes to the whole 'law and order debate', to the police and the criminal justice system. In focus group discussions in Oldtown and Bankhill there *was* criticism of all of these but this was centred on the fact that the police were not around enough, and that the criminal justice system was not hard enough on offenders. Indeed this fundamental acceptance of the need for the criminal justice system was further validated insofar as local people did become involved in local criminal justice forums.

To reiterate for example the Police Community Consultative Group meetings were attended regularly by around thirty people from Oldtown and towards sixty in the Bankhill area. These are people, then, who will criticise lack of police activity but express, in the fact of their attendance at these meetings and in their interventions that they are willing to work *with* the police to bring about change, despite the problems which this may cause them, perhaps being labelled a grass, being followed to meetings and so on. Even the school students spoken to in Bankhill, for example, had picked up on the general rhetoric, giving the solution to crime as 'more bobbies on the beat'.

The dominant discourse in these areas, then, is one of conservative values, and support, if critical, for established institutions. In reality it is the groups who are perceived to offer a challenge to existing institutions who were the most criticised in focus group discussions, the 'do-gooders' and the 'social workers' who are too soft on crime and offenders; or 'the intellectuals' who get involved in an area, without understanding it.   So whilst people might manage their relationship with criminal behaviour differently in each of the areas researched, as chapters three and four have demonstrated, there was a general commitment to the need for law and order.

A second presumption frequently made about people living in high crime areas is that they have a distinctive attitude towards criminal behaviour. With respect to this question it is important to note that in both Oldtown and Bankhill gangs of young men operated with a public profile. These gangs, the Salford Firm, the Young Firm and other, more ad hoc or family-based groupings, were certainly feared and, with justification, local residents *were* intimidated by them.

The spokesman for The Salford Firm, the gang active in Oldtown, to whom we spoke talked of the implicit acceptance and even welcoming of his gang's activities and moral code by the local community. His argument was that the Firm could put food on the tables of the poor, clothe their children cheaply, would not 'rob off their own' and could protect local people from becoming victims of crime themselves. The local 'Mr Big' would even indulge in small acts of philanthropy, 'taxing' local criminals if he is convinced that someone has become a victim of crime who should not have been so targeted, or, in one case, to give money to a local family whose belongings had been destroyed in a house fire.

This spokesman painted a picture of the area as peopled with the 'have-nots', 'people with no voice, no representatives ... the state is opposed to them - everyone's against them'. Within this there are 'the criminal class - the ones that survive by crime' and then those who would like to survive by crime - but lack the nerve.   These people will, knowingly, live off crime by buying stolen property. In this man's eyes the battle to establish alternative cultural norms is taking place and can be won by talking to those who oppose his views and explaining that the gang can make their lives better where politicians and local activists have failed.

Local people in Oldtown *do* acknowledge that the existence of this gang and its moral code does mean that, if they go along with the rules, they will feel safe from crime as chapter three has argued. However, far from winning over the hearts and minds of the majority on the estate, even those who acknowledge that they benefit from the gang's code, expressed a sense of unease that this was the case. One such man who stated that he had 'No real problems, because [he] knows people..and grew up with the local villains', nevertheless moved his teenage son out of the area after he got into trouble whilst hanging around with the local gang, in order to try to break him from a cycle of crime and drugs.

In Bankhill, where the gangs are not so well organised around a particular code, opposition to them is less ambiguous than it is in Oldtown. As one woman told us:

> They've got that strength and they can intimidate. It's up to us to have the same strength and to fight it. It's no good one person, it's no good two, it's got to be [more]. That's why they don't want to see you at meetings. (Middle aged female, established resident)

As a consequence, young people are especially to be feared in Bankhill. Moreover, for some residents the construction of their fears in this way is rooted in quite a sophisticated knowledge and experience of how youth criminality is organised in the area, as one resident, quoted earlier, stated:

> When I see blokes on bikes now, they might be innocent, but to me they're part of that gang and that's who they are, and I do not like to see anybody on a bike. (Female, established resident)

What is particularly interesting about this way of talking about crime in Bankhill is not only what it represents in terms of how people talk about their area, that is, what is present in that talk, but also what is absent from that talk. These presences and absences are in stark contrast with the presences and absences of crime talk in Oldtown. In Bankhill there is no sense of 'being alright if you're local'. People in Bankhill do not feel protected by their localness but do feel threatened and frightened by the localness of the criminality in their area. People in Oldtown, as has been argued elsewhere feel alright because they are local. This feeling does not necessarily mean they accept criminal behaviour but it does mean that they are not so uncomfortable with it. The same cannot be said for people of Bankhill.

So whilst in both of these areas there is to be found resistance to criminal behaviour, the expression and management of that resistance is differently composed. For people in Oldtown, whatever their individual attitude towards criminal behaviour it was in their collective interest to tolerate the activities of the gang. They believed that such toleration offered protection in the way that the more formal state agencies could not (like, for example, keeping 'hard' drugs off the estate) and because they knew who the criminals were they also knew how to 'manage' them. In Bankhill no such level of toleration existed. All young people were seen to be (potentially) criminal, and therefore to be feared. Focus group discussions here consistently led to the expressions of views that the police and the council could do more. Highlighting people's willingness to work with official agencies as well as their collective reluctance to work with each other.

One final presumption embedded in images of inner city life suggests that people who live in such areas are more likely to opt for the a strategy of civil disturbance rather than more conventional forms of collective political action. Again, there are many examples of community activity within Oldtown and Bankhill; for example. tenants and residents associations, bowling clubs, friendship clubs and mother and toddler groups. Within Bankhill ethnic identity played an important part in constructing community and consequently collective action. Jewish respondents repeatedly referred to their community as being able to make a difference to feelings of safety and well-being locally. They would often tell us that they knew there were local problems but that 'it is different in our community'. There was also a smaller Sikh community and Islamic mosque locally which acted as a meeting point for many of the Pakistani residents of Bankhill. Moreover within Bankhill we found a number of organisations had grown up around a collective concern and who had based their action around a particular residential grouping; for example, in target hardening housing in their area. However, this local residents association had been so intimidated by its local gang that it had ceased operating around 1992. It re-emerged soon after and at the time of the research, met covertly, outside the immediate area.

In Oldtown we found examples of collective organisation but these were more likely to have been initially set up by professionals working within the ward, rather than arising independently and as a result of resident action. As exceptions to this, however, was a long-standing tenant management co-operative as well as a local management organisation in South Oldtown. These had developed out of independent resident action and precisely in order to respond to what they saw as rising crime and incivilities within the estate.

In the South Oldtown area it was perceived police inaction which brought residents together. They had formed a 'telephone tree' so that, for example, if any resident who was part of this communication network saw a stolen car brought into the area, the telephone tree would go into operation and they were assured that a local resident would go out to deal with the incident. This collective action was later channelled into the more formal arrangement of a local management board, managing the area's council housing. But before this happened this group had decided they needed a dialogue with precisely those people on the estate who were seen to be the root of many of their problems - the disordered young men. One committee member recalled a meeting with approximately two dozen young people, mainly young men, he told us:

> ...and it was a bit overpowering to walk in there and talk to them, but I thought have a go. We had some slanging back and forwards and we told them where we were coming from and they told us where they were coming from. One thing stuck out a mile, one of them said 'It's OK for you -----, you've got a voice and you can talk to the council. The old people seem to be looked after by the council, kids get looked after by the council. Who speaks for us? If we open our mouths it's 'that so and so over there''...I said 'If you want a voice come here and I'll speak to different people'. We've worked together with the youth service. In our area it's worked, that's all we can say. (Middle aged male, established resident)

They now see themselves as having 'a working relationship' with the local youth and as having been able to put forward to young people that there is an alternative to involvement with the gangs which is more rewarding.

So whilst both of these research areas have been characterised as areas in which disturbances are most likely to occur, and have indeed experienced such disturbances, they are also areas in which other collective forms of action to deal with local problems are evident. These other forms of collective action are not necessarily connected with, nor emanate from, the statutory agencies but they are nevertheless present and work to make a difference for people involved in them.

In other words, inner city communities, can be just that, communities, in the very traditional sense of that concept, or they can be no more than spatial locations in which people live. Indeed the evidence discussed here and elsewhere in this book clearly suggests that even within traditionally understood and bounded locations there may exist a myriad possibility of diverse relationships on which policy opportunities may be differently built.   The policy possibilities and workable interventions which flow from this kind of understanding of the inner city would do well to take such variable potential into account and certainly challenge the general presumptions of those who work with an uncritical notion of the underclass on the one hand and unthinking notion of community on the other.

Understanding the 'fear of crime' debate

The implications of the findings presented in this book for the 'fear of crime' debate are relatively self-evident. Walklate (1998) has mapped the contours of that debate as comprising fear of the 'other', fear as rational and/or irrational, fear as safety and fear as anxiety. Walklate (1998) implicitly accepts the view that the notion of fear is best understood as an immediate response to a physical threat (viz. Garofalo, 1981). Consequently it is misguided to assume that it is possible to measure fear in general let alone the fear of crime in particular. Such a position has obvious implications for the criminal victimisation survey approach to measuring the 'fear of crime'. Yet the fact that such surveys have proceeded to assume that the fear of crime is measurable in the way that they have is largely explicable in terms of the embeddedness of criminology within the modernist project tied as it is to particular views of science and the policy process. Arguably it is this embeddedness which has resulted in such a partial understanding of the fear of crime and the continued commitment to measure it in some way.

Some of the shortcomings which have become embedded in the fear of crime debate have led some recent commentators to address people's concerns about crime through the concept of anxiety. On the one hand Hollway and Jefferson (1997) adopt an explicitly psychoanalytical approach. Their work reflects the presumption that anxiety is a universal feature of the human condition and their concern is to map, through the use of individual biographies, the extent to which people's expressed fear of crime (dis)connects with the mobilisation of defence mechanisms against anxiety. Their analysis reveals many and varied responses to the external threat of crime mediated by the state and status of the individual's internal threats to their sense of security.

Taylor et al. (1996) and Taylor (1996, 1997) adopt a different interpretation of anxiety. Taylor et al. (1996) use anxiety not in its psychoanalytical sense but as rooted in an exploration of locally constructed and locally understood 'structures of feeling'. Taylor (1996) develops this thesis by arguing for the need to understand the 'elective affinity' between the growth and impact of locally constructed coalition movements (Neighbourhood Watch Schemes for example) and the populations of the residential suburbs (especially in the United Kingdom). In this understanding perceptions about crime and the fear of crime become linked to peoples perceptions and experience of other kinds of 'urban fortunes'. Such perceptions are fuelled by myths and folklore rooted in what is locally known about crime in their area and simultaneously inform the management of such community safety coalitions. In this sense such structures of feeling about crime act in a metaphorical capacity for (other) related concerns about the locality.

Both these uses of anxiety display a concern with Giddens' (1991) notion of 'ontological security' and the wider context of the impact of late modern societies on individual lives. For Hollway and Jefferson (1997):

> In an age of uncertainty, discourses that appear to promise a resolution to ambivalence by producing identifiable victims and blameable villains are likely to figure prominently in the State's attempts to impose social order.

Whilst their view also presumes that the impact of those discourses may be (infinitely) individually variable, that individual variability has to be situated in the context of a late modern, risk managed society. Taylor (1997) too wishes to situate his understanding of people's expressed concerns and practices in relation to crime, in the context of the 'risk positions' in which people find themselves, though is sceptical of the ability of the risk theorists to 'recommend any public engagement (or indeed a personal praxis) with these global changes' (ibid: 60). So, to borrow a phrase from Hollway and Jefferson, though used in a rather different context, what do each of these position say in respect of what is knowable and actionable in the context of the fear of crime?

For Hollway and Jefferson the answer to this question is a matter of individual biography albeit constructed within a particular context; for Taylor it is a matter of finding a way to re-institute a conversation about the public interest albeit a locally nuanced public interest. Expressed in a different way each of these views adopt a different emphasis to the question of feeling.   Hollway and Jefferson are more about feeling than structure with the consequent problem of under-generalisability. Taylor is more about structure than feeling with the consequent problem of over-generalisability. So whilst each differently explore the paradox evidenced in the fear-risk conundrum both face the problem of establishing the validity of their particular interpretation of that evidence.

Each of these positions, then, offer us a different answer to the question of what is knowable and actionable. However, these readings of fear, emanating as they each do from the fear-risk debate, are still guided by the parameters of that debate. As a consequence these readings can only ever be partial.   The risk theorists on which they draw also talk about trust. The importance of the question of trust has been one of the key messages of the empirical findings discussed in this book.

Arguably   work   emanating   from   the   feminist   movement, especially radical feminism, has been both implicitly and explicitly concerned to problematise the question of trust in relation to women's experiences of criminal victimisation.   That work has rendered clearly problematic the notion of the safe haven of the home. Put another way, it has challenged the view that women need not fear men that they know: work colleagues, boyfriends, relatives. These were 'trustworthy' men. The view that 'All men are potential rapists' offers a definite challenge to such a presumption. The recognition that the familiar and the familial are not necessarily any more trustworthy than the stranger, puts a very different picture on the screen of who is and who is not trustworthy.   A picture which feminist research has demonstrated routinely informs women's sense of 'ontological security' (see Stanko, 1997). The question of trust, however, has largely remained absent or hidden in social scientific work in general and has been even more rarely applied to the issue of crime.

Giddens (1991) and Beck (1992) have both argued that the increasing awareness of the importance of trust is the concomitant effect of a greater awareness of the possible future damage of risk taking activity alongside the challenge to universalism posed by post-modernism. As Misztal (1996: 239) states:

> By destroying the grounds for believing in a universal truth, post-modernity does not make our lives more easy but only less constrained by rules and more contingent. It demands new solutions based on the tolerant co-existence of a diversity of cultures.   Yet although post

modernism encourages us to live without an enemy, it stops short of offering constructive bases for mutual understanding and trust.

In order to 'live without an enemy', however, requires trust. But how does trust manifest itself? The comparative data generated by the research project discussed in this book also supports the usefulness of exploring the mechanism of trust which underpin people's sense of ontological security in high crime areas. The value of this has been suggested by the notion of a 'square of trust' (see chapters three and four). The actual manifestation of this square of trust may be differently mediated by the nature of community relationships, age, gender, ethnicity etc., all of which are discussed elsewhere (ibid.). Those mediations suggest that there may be key mechanisms through which it may be possible to understand individual and collective expressions of 'ontological security'. These relationships can be expressed, analytically, in the following way.

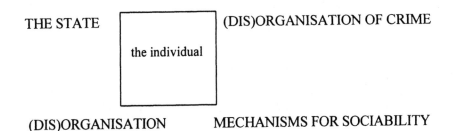

THE STATE   the individual   (DIS)ORGANISATION OF CRIME

(DIS)ORGANISATION OF COMMUNITY   MECHANISMS FOR SOCIABILITY

Figure 4   The Square of Trust

In this square of trust, whom you can trust, how you trust and how much you can trust (Nelken, 1994) at an individual level depend upon where an individual is located between these mechanisms. To reiterate, based on our fieldwork in Oldtown, it would appear that people trust as much as the local neighbourhood dogma permits whilst simultaneously endeavouring to avoid 'public shaming' (being labelled a 'grass'). This takes the form, primarily of trusting other local people, because they are local (mechanisms of sociability). This does not mean, however, that other individuals are not trusted. But those others are trusted in a highly individualistic and fragile manner and that trust is dependent upon what those individuals do with the trust invested in them.   This may, for example, include trusting individual police officers and individual officials from other agencies, but it certainly does not mean offering generalised trust to those official agencies (the state).   The risks of 'public shaming' are too high a price to pay for whatever benefits might accrue from such a co-operative venture.   These processes do not mean, however, that the anarchistic politics of the presence of criminal gangs (organised crime) have won the hearts and minds of this community (as indicated above) But it does mean that we may have to re-think some of the mechanisms whereby social solidarity is produced and maintained (the organised nature of the community).

Trusting relationships look somewhat different, however, in Bankhill. The responses here appear to suggest that older people are still willing to offer a generalised trust to the 'official agencies' (the state) and that there are friendship and community groups which strive to offer some kind of militation against a totally atomised existence (mechanisms of sociability).   However, the belief that 'This area is going downhill rapidly' (the level of disorganisation in the community) and the expressed fears of young people (the disorganised nature of local crime) undermine the sense of belonging on which the potential for trusting relationships inherent in the call for help from 'the officials' might be developed. Thus there is an absence of social solidarity and a withdrawal from the processes on which such solidarity might be predicated. For younger people in this community the picture is somewhat different. They know they cannot be seen to be talking to 'officials' (the state), which for them might include older people. They also know that to stay out of trouble of different kinds they have to manage the tightrope of being known (their mechanisms of sociability), but not being a 'grass', nor participating in criminal activity (the disorganised nature of crime). For them, living in their locality was no worse than anywhere else and trust exists between those who know each other, but not much beyond.

The different ways in which the questions of who do you trust, when do you trust, how much do you trust, manifest themselves in the discussion above may be rooted in the different histories of the two areas which were investigated. However, whilst that trust may be rooted in history, it is not historical. It is a real mechanism whereby individuals create a way of managing their routine daily lives, which differently situates them in relation to the state, crime, community, and social relationships. The extent to which individuals express fear or not can be understood by reference to their location in relation to these general mechanisms. The implications of thinking about the lived experience of high crime areas in this way are substantial not only in political and policy terms but also in relation to how we talk about and understand the fear of crime. Such an understanding is manifested in both the presences and absences in talk about crime alongside the commission and omission of action with respect to crime. These processes are again more often than not locally constructed and locally nuanced and raise questions about the nature of policy and the policy implementation process, the third dimension to be discussed here.

Whose policy? Whose process?

To reiterate, the two areas under investigation during the course of this research were less than two miles apart, yet it is from the findings which have been presented, that the question of what might work in each of these areas looks (potentially) very different; so what might that look like?

Partnership has become the new buzzword of the crime prevention industry; a buzzword which has become tied to the notion of community. Crawford (1997) has situated the appeals to 'community' and 'partnership' in the wider processes of the governance of crime; that is, as part of the increasingly shifting boundaries between the state and other inter/intra organisational networks (the public, the private, the voluntary sector etc..) Analyses of the partnership approach such as these make sense if, and only if, researchers and policy makers alike insist on looking for solutions to the crime problem from the top down; but when an analysis looks from the bottom up (Lewis and Salem, 1986), the question is raised as to whether community safety partnerships can prevent, reduce or manage crime in areas like Oldtown and Bankhill? If so, how and under what circumstances? As this question has been more fully discussed in Chapter Four we shall re-visit it only briefly here.

To recap: in Bankhill, there was a willingness and desire to work with the 'authorities' and there was a trust and expectation invested in those 'authorities' to make things happen in return. There, people wanted their concerns, which may appear petty and trivial, to be taken seriously by the 'authorities'. Consequently, in an area like this, the local authority and the police may be able to take a lead in local developments and will find support for such in the local community; though that support may lead to a broader interpretation of the notion of partnership above and beyond the usual multi-agency approach. This vision of partnership implies a view of crime as a local problem to be managed locally, not necessarily prevented or reduced.

On the other hand, in Oldtown, arguably, the problem was already being managed, not by a community safety partnership strategy as such, but through the (fragile) equilibrium which exists between the police, the local community and the organised nature of crime in that area. A very different conception of what might constitute a partnership! Yet the processes underpinning these relationships, in allowing people to feel all right about living in their locality, seemed to work for most of the people living there most of the time. Simultaneously partnerships may well be formed in areas like Oldtown but such partnerships may not have any of the characteristics of more conventional organisational allegiances. Such partnerships may be, for example, with strategically placed individual residents. Strategically placed individuals who may be influential in carrying other local people with them. Here again the result may not be crime prevention or crime reduction, but crime management with the opportunity of maintaining and/or restoring local equilibrium or at least offering an opportunity to discover what that might look like.

The implications of this discussion suggest that it is necessary to move away from either universalistic and/or simplistic solutions to crime in localities like Oldtown and Bankhill. The alternatives may be more complex (though not necessarily more expensive); they may have different outcomes than those valued by the crime prevention industry; and they may challenge conventional views of what is, or is not, acceptable as a crime problem. In addition they raise the questions of not only whose policy and whose process is crime prevention but also the question of what is democratically acceptable at a local as well as a national level. Locally informed and locally formulated policy responses may need to take count of the diversity of views which exist and which are acceptable. Moreover the meaning of 'locally' may need to be re-interpreted and re-defined in terms of quite small units (maybe at the level of street in some localities) in order to formulate policies which make sense to local people and therefore stand a chance of working.

Conclusion: Citizen, State, Market and Policy

Oldtown and Bankhill are not unusual places. Each urban (and increasingly rural) area has their equivalent Oldtowns and Bankhills. These are predominantly white areas, where the traditional working class historically co-existed with the 'social scum' alongside those who were endeavouring to better themselves as market forces permitted. Oldtown and Bankhill may be at different points on a socio-economic trajectory (which this research was not designed to accommodate); but this trajectory is suggestive (almost) of an ecological, historically driven, process which Oldtown has found a way of managing and Bankhill is in the process of so doing. Such a process is characterised by a number of features; one of which is understanding the changing mechanisms of social inclusion and exclusion, especially in a context in which the nature of work is changing.

Evans, Fraser, and Walklate (1996: 379) state:

> ... your *place* in relation to crime *places* you in a community of belonging and exclusion ... It is consequently important to recognise who is seen to be protecting you and how: for many people it is not the police or the council but local families and/or the Salford Firm. Moreover, it is the absence of confidence in the formal agencies which creates the space for those other forces to come into play.

This quote refers to Oldtown; a locality from which the state had, for the most part, withdrawn. It was apparent that parts of Bankhill were also in the process of suffering a similar fate. There are other similar localities throughout the United Kingdom, as Campbell's (1993) analysis suggests; some of them peopled by ethnic minorities; just as many peopled by Caucasians. They are all areas which have been left behind by the market forces of the last two decades. These are the locations which have suffered disproportionately as the gap between rich and poor has grown and as we have become increasingly a 30/30/40 society (Hutton, 1995). To reiterate, a critical reflection on the findings produced by this research reveals much about the ways in which the mechanisms of social inclusion and exclusion have operated and been managed at a local level. The question remains as to how much responsibility we should assume, collectively, for the most vulnerable in our society, however we might choose to define that vulnerability.

It is clear that whilst the relationship between the citizen and the state has changed in emphasis in the U.K. since 1945; there are also strong historical continuities in that relationship. Historical continuities informed by notions of a distinction between the deserving and undeserving, the principle of less eligibility, and the notion of the dangerous classes. These dangerous classes, of course, provide the criminal justice system with much of its work so for that reason alone it is important to grasp a clear understanding of how and why that these processes happen in the way that they do.

In a different context Currie (1997) has discussed the marketization of violence. By that he is referring to the processes whereby the 'pursuit of private gain' is 'likely to breed high levels of violent crime'. In this context, that same pursuit seems to have produced communities which, when left to devise their own management strategies, have found ways of making life all right for themselves: the marketization of trust. The consequences of these processes are there to be seen (inter alia) in the Social Exclusion Report referred to at the beginning of this chapter. That report highlights communities, notably including Salford, for whom not only crime, but health, education, housing etc., still constitute issues for serious concern. In the forward to that document the Prime Minister states:

> Our goal is simple: to bridge the gap between the poorest neighbourhoods and the rest of Britain. Bridging that gap will not be easy. It will require imagination, persistence, and commitment.

The research discussed here certainly supports the view that bridging this gap will not be easy. Those who are socially excluded, and have found ways of managing that exclusion, will not be easily persuaded that it is in their interests to manage differently.

At the time of writing, as is illustrated in the Introduction to this book, local authorities were being required to engage in Crime Audits with a view to developing local partnerships as a way of tackling local crime problems. These requirements have been put in place by the Crime and Disorder Act 1998. That legislation is wide in its coverage. One of its key concerns is also to address the problem of young people and crime. That concern is reflected in the desire to render the criminal justice process swifter in its handling of young offenders and more meaningful. This latter concern is present in the aforementioned legislation in the form of the concept of reparation. Given the problematic status accorded to young people in the findings presented from this investigation, the question of whether or not the strategy proposed by the Crime and Disorder Act will work is of particular interest. It is perhaps worth reiterating the relevance of these research findings to this question once again especially with respect to the question of young offenders.

The partnership approach in tackling all kinds of crime has been well-embraced in policy thinking. For example, the Audit Commission (1996) recognised the importance of understanding and working with the interconnections between the family, school, local authorities and the criminal justice system in dealing with the problem of young people (young men) and crime. The potential value, or otherwise, of reparation has also been well established. As this research as demonstrated, however, what can be understood by the term partnership is wide and varied, and how such partnerships might work is also wide and varied. For example, in Oldtown, it is possible to argue that partnership and reparation already exists. Young people who step over the boundaries of what is considered to be acceptable criminality in this area are quicly made to see the error of their ways through various shaming mechanisms from being labelled a 'grass' or being 'taxed', to more physical forms of punishment. Such mechanisms may not be what the professionals have in mind when they talk of 'reintegrative shaming' (Braithwaite, 1989), but they are public and they do seem to work. How might the Crime and Disorder Act improve on this for the people of Oldtown? In Bankhill, however, the fluidity of social relationships suggests that there is much more room for manoeuvre and meaningful inter-agency work around these issues.

So, the question remains as to whether or not the proposed policy strategies to tackle this issue are imaginative, persistent and committed enough to face this social reality, 'to think the unthinkable', and work with that in a meaningful way; since this research also clearly demonstrates that there are opportunities there for that to happen. If the lived experiences of those people living in high crime areas are taken into account, there is clearly another layer of questions to be considered concerning what works, for whom, how, why, where and when. However in order for such accounting to occur it is important that academics, politicians, policy makers and the locally powerful pay constant vigilant attention to the questions of whose policy and whose community. As Giddens (1998:88) states:

> In order to work, partnerships between government agencies, the criminal justice system, local associations and community organisations have to be inclusive - all economic and ethnic groups must be involved. ... To be successful, such schemes demand a long-term commitment to social objectives.

As he goes on to point out, such an approach neither necessarily means that any link between unemployment, poverty and crime is denied; but it does mean that policies need to be co-ordinated with common goals and objectives. They also need to be resourced: an issue remarkably absent from the implementation process of the Crime and Disorder Act.

However, to reiterate, above all, a genuine desire for policy to work for change needs to be cognisant of the importance of the local context in which that policy is set. This desire needs to work with rather than against the historical and socio-economic circumstances which structure that local context. Such a desire does demand imagination, commitment and persistence. It also requires that desire for policy to work to be both authentic and genuine for the communities themselves.

Appendix One: Research Methodology

When this project was conceived initially its concerns were centrally located within the 'fear of crime' debate. That debate, arguably, has moved through a number of phases over the last twenty five years; from the fears constructed in relation to the perceived rising phenomenon of 'black crime' in the 1970s, to the questioned rationality and /or irrationality of people's fears characteristic of the debate during the 1980s, to the more focused attention on community safety in the 1990s. In the context of that changing debate this project sought to situate an understanding of the 'risk from' and 'fear of' crime in a comparative local urban context. We wanted to understand how people who lived, worked, and went to school in these localities constructed their own responses to such 'risks' and 'fears'. The research had five main objectives:

1. to document and analyse lay perceptions of 'risk' and 'safety' within these two locations in a variety of social contexts; on the street, in the workplace, at school, at home.
2. to document and analyse professional perceptions of 'risk' and 'safety' within these two communities.
3. to document and evaluate the nature of formal policy interventions in these two communities.
4. document and evaluate the informal policy processes in these two communities.
5. to assess the future trajectory of policy processes.

Given these objectives the research process itself used a range of different research techniques. As we were concerned to explore the 'lived realities' (Genn, 1988) of the people in these two locations the research process research techniques. As we were concerned to explore the 'lived realities' (Genn, 1988) of the people in these two locations the research process

143

endeavoured to obtain a feel for and remain sensitive to local issues as local people experienced them. To this end the research, informed by the ideas of methodological pluralism, reflects an empirical strategy which deployed both qualitative and quantitative techniques as appropriate. It is important to note two features of the research team itself which added their own level of significance to the research process.

1. All the members of the research team were female. In relation to the kind of work being proposed and the nature of the projects funded under this particular ESRC Initiative this was unusual. Given the nature of some of the issues which came to light during the course of this project, especially to the importance attached to the presence of the criminal gang in Oldtown, this all-female research team certainly posed no disadvantages, and was, arguably advantageous.

2. All the members of the research team had pre-existing connections with the locations under investigation; one had lived in one of the research areas for three years, one engaged in voluntary work in one of the locations, and one had formal links with those charged with the responsibility for implementing community safety strategies. All of these links equipped the team with different levels of prior knowledge about the locations under study, some of which certainly facilitated access.

The first six months of the project were spent gaining an in-depth knowledge of both the areas by interviewing professional and semi-professional workers in both locations, through ethnographic work (walking around the areas, going to the pubs, going to local meetings), and regular analysis of the local newspapers. Twenty-six interviews were completed with 29 professional and semi-professional workers in each of the areas. From this knowledge we were able to build a detailed picture of each of the locations; a knowledge which formed the backlcoth against which we conducted our house to house survey of residents. The conduct of that survey built on this knowledge in several particular ways.

The criminal victimisation survey which we conducted comprised tried and tested questions taken from pre-existing criminal victimisation surveys amended to take account of our own more localised concerns. It was administered by a groups of Salford University students working in pairs, trained by ourselves, to take account of local police advice on such work in these locations and being mindful of the experience of a Home Office sponsored survey conducted a few months earlier. The interviewers were not stereotypical university students. They were all mature with northern connections; some were from Salford itself. And although they were going into houses with traditional survey instruments we ensured that this process was delivered in a particular way. We trained the interviewers to pay particular attention to the importance of informality and of asking questions as if they were a part of a conversation. We asked them to be fairly informal in their dress and not to carry clip boards or briefcases but to carry the questionnaires around in plastic bags. this was done as a way of trying to increase their safety on the streets as well as helping the respondent feel more relaxed and confident about the process.

The survey's sampling technique was one which might be called a targeted random sample. Our initial work in these two locations had alerted us to the way in which each of the areas under investigation was differently structured for the people who were living and working there. In other words, from the information gathered during our six months ethnographic work we learned that it was possible to identify 9 smaller identifiable localities in Oldtown and 13 in Bankhill. As a result the individuals who actually participated in our survey were chose at random but in a context in which we had purposefully ensured that each identifiable locality was equally represented. This process generated a total of 596 completed interviews (we had a target of 600 completed interviews). We engaged in interviewing at different points in time during the day and during the week and the actual sample generated came very close to the demographic profile of the area.

One of the purposes of the house to house survey was to identify local people who might be willing to participate in focus group discussions and also to inform how those focus groups might be constructed. On the basis of this we held focus group discussions in Oldtown which included 21 residents and in Bankhill which included 29 residents during the next six months.

Following on from this work we identified three localities in each ward as 'typical case' studies for further in-depth work. In each of these localities we sent out a postal questionnaire to all the businesses, and other organisations in existence there with a view to capturing a picture of their experiences of working in these areas. A total of 100 community groups and 219 businesses were contacted. These contacts were supplemented with telephone interviews with respondents where there was an expressed willingness on the part of the respondents to do this.

In parallel with this activity we collected and analysed police command and control data for our two research areas for the month of January 1995, and conducted in-depth interviews and focus group work with officers patrolling these two wards. This involved a total of 18 officers of varying ranks.

In addition we held eight focus group discussions with 13-15 year olds in each of the local secondary schools.

Ethnographic work continued throughout the course of the study exemplified by regular attendance at police-community consultative meetings, other local fora as well as continued analysis of the local press. Wherever possible in the last six months of the work we attended local policy group meetings both to disseminate our initial findings and also as a means of establishing some critical feedback on our work.

Commentary

Whilst the preceding discussion offers an overall descriptive outline of what was done and what those practices were concerned to address what it does not capture in the process which took place. That process is an important dimension to any research project and is often difficult to capture on reflection. However, there are a number of important elements to the process which took place during the course of this research project which it is important to comment upon.

The interaction between empirical discovery and conceptual development

As was stated at the beginning of this Appendix this research began itself concretely situated within the 'fear of crime' debate and for the first six months of its life that debate continued to fuel its concerns. However, a significant moment of change occurred during the conduct of the criminal victimisation survey. This survey was conducted in parallel in Oldtown and Bankhill during the months of August/ September 1994. During the course of that process the student interviewers, who were debriefed after every session of interviewing, reported to us that the survey appeared to be working in Bankhill but not Oldtown. When pressed further as to what was meant by this the students told us that people in Oldtown were saying that the questions we were asking did not make any sense to them because 'you were alright round here if you were local'. The students had been instructed to record any response they received to the questions asked whether or not they matched a particular category and it became clear that this sense of being 'alright' was being offered often enough for us to re-think whether or not our conceptual apparatus was appropriate. A return to some of the more qualitative interview and ethnographic work, alongside this response to some of the survey questions led us to consider the extent to which the concept of trust might be a more useful analytical tool than those we had originally adopted. On further analysis we are happier with what this kind of analytical framework can reveal about how people manage their lives in high crime areas than that proffered by either the notions of 'fear', 'risk', or 'safety'.

The serendipity of empirical information

Again, as the description of the research process offered here implies, this work was primarily conceived in terms of people's experiences of crime and criminal victimisation. We had not originally envisaged being concerned with offending behaviour per se nor with offenders. However a shooting incident in Bankhill during the course of conducting our survey, led to a minor local demonstration about the police conduct of this incident which subsequently established, in a very clear way, the role and importance of one criminal gang in particular. The nature of the local knowledge and contacts of one of the researchers led to a very useful interview with the spokesperson for this criminal gang and provided a further, and unpredicted, important source of information about the nature of crime and criminal victimisation, especially in Oldtown. The importance of that information was subsequently validated by the data we gathered from the businesses in that location. Given that this was not a piece of research concerned centrally with the nature of criminal gang activity the opportunities for exploring this dimension of life in these two areas was not taken further. Arguably however, without the local acceptability of one of the researchers, the sex of the research team, and the particular incident which occurred, the importance of this aspect of community life in these two areas may not have been grasped.

Exploring conceptual subtleties

When this research was originally conceived, and the research proposal initially put together (1993) little attention had been paid to the viability or otherwise of the concept of victim or victimisation. Broadly put, there existed considerable tension between victimology's use of the term 'victim' and the feminist use of the term 'survivor'. These two terms are in some respects also reflected in the conceptual usage of 'fear' or 'safety'.   One of the more hidden dimensions to the empirical investigation which is the focus of concern here is the way in which, especially during focus group discussion, the subtleties of such terms can be more clearly identified. Arguably, this is in part a product of the focus group technique in which group discussion is guided but never led. In that context we could identify people who were not victims, but felt themselves to be, people who were victims and did not see themselves in those terms, and organisations who were both seen to be and were actually victims rather victimisers.   This aspect of the research process would benefit from further exploration. It is clear, however, that without the use of the focus group technique a good deal of subtle, nuanced understanding would have been lost.

Controlling dissemination

Part of the research process as described above was very much concerned with dissemination. To this end we allocated six months of the research time to this and produced two reports, one for Oldtown and one for Bankhill which were distributed to all who had participated in the research and which were made freely available to any appropriate local forum. Our research findings were used by:

> Ordsall Safety Task Group, January 1996
> Community Strategy Consultative Committee, November 1995
> Community Strategy Youth Task Group, Broughton, November 1995
> Planning Division, City Technical Services, City of Salford, February 1996

In addition we were invited to submit proposals in the City of Salford's bid for single regeneration monies - their bid for SRB2 monies included one of the areas in which we were working. This bid was successful and we maintained a dialogue with local councillors concerning the further development of this work and in January 1996 we gave a presentation to the City Council's Corporate Risk Management Group on the findings of our research.

Despite all these efforts, and the goodwill which we felt had been established during this process, a report produced in the local press in the summer of 1996 significantly soured these relationships. Our first article from the research was published in the Sociological Review in August of that year and a conscientious local reporter read it and produced a rather more sensational newspaper article on its contents. Needless to say that newspaper reporting paid significantly more attention to the presence and impact of the criminal gang in one of our localities much to the chagrin of the City Council. No amount of persuasion would convince the officers of the council that we had played no part in this process and letters were exchanged between the City Council, the ESRC and the Director of the Initiative under which this research had been funded. It reminded the researchers of the old adage from Howard Becker that a good piece of research will make someone angry. It was fortuitous that the month of August 1996 also saw the end of the project.

This event, however, reminded the research team in a very real way of the sensitivity and the sensibilities involved in engaging in research of this kind. It is important to be mindful that people who live in high crime areas can feel victimised by the research whose intentions might be to improve things for and with them and that there are greater, usually economic interests at stake for the locally powerful trying to bring business and work to an area. To deny the problems which exist, however, is not perhaps the best way of addressing these sensibilities; but to look for the possibilities which exist for change, which hopefully this book has demonstrated might be a more useful option.

Appendix Two:
The Questionnaire

COMMUNITY SAFETY IN SALFORD

Questionnaire Number

Interviewer

House/Flat Number

Street

Date   Length of time of interview

YOUR LOCAL AREA

To begin with could you mark on this map where you consider is your local area?

1.   Could I ask you how long you have lived in this area?

2. SHOWCARD 1
        Which of these terms would you use to describe your local area?

        A - it has a community feel
        B - it is a friendly area
        C - it is going downhill
        D - it is a good area to live in
        E - it is improving
        F - it does not look nice
        G - it is an area with a lot of problems

        H - Don't know
        I - No response
        J - None of these

    Any other comments:

3. SHOWCARD 2
        What are the best things about living in this area?

        A - the people
        B - the housing
        C - it looks nice
        D - there are parks and greenery
        E - the schools
        F - job opportunities
        G - the community
        H - the local shops

        I - Don't know
        J - No response
        K - None of these

    Any other comments:

4. SHOWCARD 3

> Could you tell us which of the following you think are a problem in your local area? Please tell us whether you think each one is either (1) a big problem, (2) a problem, or (3) not a problem, in your local area?

(1)   (2)   (3)

> A - Lack of public transport
> B - Unfriendly people
> C - Vandalism
> D - Harassment or unwanted
>   comments towards women
> E - Unemployment
> G - Graffiti
> H - Nowhere for children to play
> I - Poor housing
> J - Crime
> K - Young people hanging about
> L - Poor street lighting
> M - Noisy neighbours
> N - Harassment or insults to do
>   with someone's race or colour
>
> O - Don't know
> P - No response
> Q - None of these
>
> Any others:

5. Which, if any, is the biggest problem *for you*?

6. Over the last few weeks has anything happened which has influenced the way you feel about this problem?

PERSONAL SAFETY

7. SHOWCARD 4
During the day-time, in your local area, do you ever worry about?

A - Using public transport
B - Being out on your own
C - Being burgled
D - Being bothered by groups of young people
E - Your property being vandalised
F - Being attacked by strangers
G - Being attacked by someone you know
H - Your car being stolen
I - Being robbed in the street
J - Being pestered or harassed
K - Being raped or sexually assaulted
L - Walking past pubs

M - Don't know
N - No response
O - None of these

Anything else:

8. SHOWCARD 4
When it is dark, in your local area, do you ever worry about?

A - Using public transport
B - Being out on your own
C - Being burgled
D - Being bothered by groups of young people
E - Your property being vandalised
F - Being attacked by strangers
G - Being attacked by someone you know
H - Your car being stolen
I - Being robbed in the street
J - Being pestered or harassed

K - Being raped or sexually assaulted
L - Walking past pubs

M - Don't know
N - No response
O - None of these

Anything else:

9.   Would you say your local area is?

A - very safe
B - quite safe
C - neither safe nor unsafe
D - quite unsafe
E - very unsafe

F - don't know
G - no response
H - None of these

Any other comments:

10.   Do you think your local area is?

A - not as safe as it used to be
B - about the same as always
C - safer than it used to be

D - don't know
E - no response
F - None of these

Any other comments:

11.   Are there any parts of Oldtown/Bankhill where you feel less safe
        than others?

        A - Yes
        B - No (Go to Question 16)

12.   Where are these parts and why do you think you feel like this
        about these places?

        Where   Why

        ....

        ....

13.   Do you ever have to go through these places?

        A - Yes
        B - No (Go to Question 16)

14. SHOWCARD 6
        What do you do to reassure or to protect yourself?

        A - walk quickly
        B - go with someone else
        C - drive
        D - carry a weapon
        E - carry a personal alarm
        F - walk in the middle of the street
        G - take the dog

        H - Don't know
        I - No response
        J - None of these

        Anything else:

YOUNG PEOPLE'S SAFETY

15.   Do you have any children?

       A - Yes
       B - No (Go to Question 20)

16.   Can I ask what age they are and whether you have sons or
       daughters?

       Sons   Daughters
       Age(s)...................................   Age(s).................

ASK ONLY THOSE WITH CHILDREN BETWEEN THE AGES OF 13
AND 15 INC.

ALL OTHERS GO TO QUESTION 20

17. SHOWCARD 7

When your children are at school do you worry about any of the following happening to them?

ASK ABOUT SONS AND DAUGHTERS SEPARATELY

	Sons	Daughters

A - Being bullied
B - Being taxed
C - Being harmed on the roads
D - Being abducted
E - Being attacked by other young people
F - Being offered alcohol/drinking
G - Being offered cigarettes/smoking
H - Being offered drugs/taking drugs
I - Hanging around with the wrong people
J - Getting pregnant
K - Joyriding
L - Playing in dangerous places
M - Being sexually attacked or pestered
N - Getting into trouble with the police
O - Getting into fights

P - Don't know   Q - No response   R - None of these

Anything else:

18. SHOWCARD 7

When your children are out with their friends, do you worry about any of the following happening to them.

ASK ABOUT SONS AND DAUGHTERS SEPARATELY

Sons   Daughters

A - Being bullied
B - Being taxed
C - Being harmed on the roads
D - Being abducted
E - Being attacked by other young people
F - Being offered alcohol/drinking
G -Being offered cigarettes/smoking
H -Being offered drugs/taking drugs
I - Hanging around with the wrong people
J - Getting pregnant
K - Joyriding
L - Playing in dangerous places
M - Being sexually attacked or pestered
N - Getting into trouble with the police
O - Getting into fights

P - Don't know
Q - No response
R - None of these - being bullied

Anything else:

19.   What sort of advice would you give to a daughter to keep her safe?

20.   What sort of advice would you give to a son to keep him safe?

FEAR OF CRIME

21.   Thinking back over the last 5 years, do you think the level of
        crime in this neighbourhood has.............?

        A - gone up
        B - gone down
        C - stayed the same

        D - Don't know
        E - No response
        F - None of these

        Any other comments:

22.   What sort of crimes do you think have increased?

23.   What sort of crimes do you think have decreased?

24.   How do you think that crime in this area compares to other parts of Salford and the UK?

                                                  Salford   UK

A - It's about average
B - It's one of the worst areas
C - It's one of the best areas
D - Don't know
E - No response
F - None of these

Any other comments:

25.   Could you think back for a moment to this time last year? In the last year has a crime been committed against you personally?

A - Yes
B - No (Go to Question 29)

26.   May I ask what that was? (record all)

i) ....

ii) ....

iii)...

iv)...

v)..

27. SHOWCARD 8

Have you seen any of the following take place in this area?

A - Burglary
B - Joyriding
C - Groups of young people harassing people
D - A woman being attacked by a man
E - A break-in at a shop or workplace
F - Fights in the streets
G - People taking drugs
H - People selling drugs
I - Glue sniffing
J - Vandalism of property or cars
K - People carrying a knife or other weapon
L - Dogs fighting

M - Don't know
N - No response
O - None of these

Anything else:

28. SHOWCARD 9

Which of the following do you think is a problem in your area?

A - Drunk driving
B - Shoplifting
C - Joy riding
D - Violence against women
E - People taking drugs
F - Burglary from businesses
G - Police behaviour
H - Drug dealing
I - Domestic disputes
J - Criminal gangs
K - Car theft or break-ins

L - Burglary from homes
M - Protection rackets

N - Don't know
O - No response
P - None of these

Anything else:

COMMUNITY SAFETY MEASURES

29. SHOWCARD 10

Can you tell us which of the following you think is important for ensuring safety in the home? Please tell us whether you think each one is (1) very important, (2) important or, (3) not important:

(1)   (2)   (3)

A - Burglar alarms
B - Good locks
C - Street lighting
D - Good neighbours
E - Neighbourhood Watch
F - Stronger doors
G - Door-entry phones
H - Secure garden walls or fencing
I - Street patrols
J - Having an ex-directory
      phone number
K - Don't know
L - No response
M - None of these

Any others:

30. SHOWCARD 11

In the same way, can you tell us which of the following you think are important for ensuring your safety outside the home?

A - Street lighting
B - Busy streets
C - Carrying personal alarms
D - Not carrying money around
E - Sticking to places you know
F - Knowing how to defend yourself

G - Not going anywhere on your own
H - Taking a dog with you

I - Don't know
J - No response
K - None of these

Any others:

ABOUT YOU

31. SH CARD 12
    Do you belong to any of the following groups?

    A - Mother and toddler group
    B - Tenant's assoc
    C - Resident's assoc
    D - Church/Temple
    E - Neighbourhood Watch
    F - Babysitting rotas
    G - Women's group
    H - Trade union
    I - Local history group
    J - Parents/Teachers assoc

    Any others:

32. SHOWCARD 13
    Do you use the following?

    A - Local sports clubs
    B - local libraries
    C - local pubs
    D - local community centres
    E - local youth clubs
    F - (Oldtown only) Resource Centre or Job Shop
    G - local social clubs
    H - local church/temple
    I - local shops

    Any other facilities:

33.   Do most of your family or friends live in this area as well?

    A - Yes
    B - No

34.   Do you ....?
    (FILL IN AS MANY AS APPLY)

    A - rent from a housing association
    B - rent from private landlord
    C - rent from the council
    D - own your home
    E - lodge with a friend
    F - live with your family

    Any other:

35. SHOWCARD

How would your household be placed if you suddenly had to find a sum of money to meet an unexpected expense, for example a repair or a washing machine? Please look at this card and tell us which amounts would be.......

	Not a problem	A bit of a problem	Quite a problem	A huge problem
1st				
2nd				
3rd				
4th				
5th				
6th				

36.   Which of these age groups do you belong to?

A - 16 - 24
B - 25 - 44
C - 45 - 64
D - 65 - 74
E - 75 +

37.   How would you describe your ethnic origin?

38.   What is your occupation?

39.   Are you...............?
A - single
B - married
C - living with someone
D - divorced
E - widowed
F - separated
G - living with your parents

Other:

40.   DO NOT ASK
       Is the respondent....?

       A - Male
       B - Female

41.   We would like to invite you to take part in the next stage of the
       research, could we have your name so that we can contact you
       again?

       Name ....

THANK YOU

Bibliography

Anderson, E. (1990), *Streetwise: Race, Class and Change in an Urban Community*, University of Chicago Press, Chicago.

Audit Commission (1996), *Misspent Youth*, The Audit Commission, London.

Barke, M. and Turnbull G. (1992), *Meadowell: The Biography of an 'Estate With Problems'*, Avebury, Aldershot.

Beck, U. (1992), *The Risk Society*, Sage, London.

Bottoms, A.E. (1990), 'Crime Prevention Facing the 1990s', *Policing and Society*, vol. 1, no. 1, pp. 3-22.

Braithewaite, J. (1989), *Crime, Shame and Reintegration*, Oxford University Press, Oxford.

Bratton, W. (1997), *Zero Tolerance: Policing a Free Society*, Institute for Economic Affairs, London.

Brownill, S. (1993), 'The Docklands Experience: Locality and Community in London' in R. Imrie and H. Thomas (eds), *British Urban Policy and the Urban Development Corporations*, Paul Chapman, Liverpool.

Burrows, R. and Rhodes, D. (1998), 'Unpopular Places? Area Disadvantage and the Geography of Misery in England', Joseph Rowntree Foundation.

Caine, J. (1992), 'Matchstalk Men on Song', The Observer, 10th October.

Campbell, B. (1993), *Goliath: Britain's Dangerous Places*, Methuen, London.

City of Salford (1994), *Community Strategy*.

Coleman, A. (1990), *Utopia on Trial: Vision and Reality in Planned Housing*, H. Shipman, London.

Cramphorn, C. (1994), Presentation to Witness Intimidation Seminar, Worsley, Salford, November.

Crawford, A. (1994), 'The Partnership Approach to Community Crime Prevention: Corporatism at the Local Level?', *Social and Legal Studies*, vol. 3, pp. 497-519.

Crawford, A. (1997), *The Governance of Crime*, Clarendon, Oxford.

Crow, G. and Allan, G. (1994), *Community Life: An Introduction to Local Social Relations*, Harvester Wheatsheaf, Hemel Hempstead.

Currie, E. (1997), 'Market, Crime and Community: Toward a Mid-range Theory of Post-Industrial Violence', *Theoretical Criminology*, vol.1, no. 2, pp. 147-72.

Davies, A. (1987), 'Saturday Night Markets in Manchester and Salford 1840-1939', *Manchester Region History Review*, vol. 1, no. 2.

Day, G. and Murdoch, J. (1993), 'Locality and community: coming to terms with place', *Sociological Review* , vol. 41, no. 1, pp. 82-111.

Delaney, S. (1982), *A Taste of Honey*, London, Methuen.

Engels, F. (1958), *The Conditions of the Working Class in England*, Basil Blackwell, Oxford.

Erikson, K.T. (1966), *Wayward Puritans,* John Wiley, New York.

Etzioni, A. (1996), *The Spirit of Community: The Re-invention of American Society,* Simon and Schuster, New York.

European Union (1997), *Criminal Victimisation in Eleven Industrialised Countries, Key Findings from the 1996 International Crime Victimisation Survey*, Noordwjik, Netherlands.

Evans, K. (1997), '"It's Alright Round Here If You're Local" - Community in the Inner City' in P. Hogget, (ed), *Contested Communities,* Policy Press, Bristol.

Evans, K. and Walklate, S. (1996), 'Community Safety, Personal Safety and the Fear of Crime', *End of Project Report*, ESRC.

Evans, K., and Walklate, S. (1997), *Policetalk About Crime in High Crime Areas*, paper presented to the British Criminology Conference, July, Belfast.

Evans, K., Fraser, P. and Walklate, S. (1996), 'Grassing: Whom Do You Trust in the Inner City?', *Sociological Review*, vol. 44, no. 3.

Forrest, R. and Gordon, D. (1993), *People and Places: A 1991 Census Atlas of England*, University of Bristol, SAUS Publications, Bristol.

Fraser, P. (1997), 'Social and Spatial Relationships and the "Problem" Inner City. Moss Side in Manchester', *Critical Social Policy*, vol. 16, no. 4.

Fukuyama, F. (1996), *Trust: The Social Virtues and the Creation of Prosperity*, Penguin, London.

Garland, D. (1996), 'The limits of the sovereign state: strategies of crime control in contemporary societies', *British Journal of Criminology,* vol. 36, no. 4, pp. 445-71.

Garofalo, J. (1981), 'The Fear of Crime: Causes and Consequences', *Journal of Criminal Law and Criminal Policy,* no. 72, pp. 839-957.

Garrard, J.A. and Goldsmith, M. (1970) *Salford Elections. 1919-1969* Department of Sociology, Government and Administration, University of Salford.

Gellner, E. (1989), 'Trust, Cohesion, and the Social Order' in D. Gambetta (ed.), *Trust: Making and Breaking Co-operative Relations,* Basil Blackwell, London.

Genn, H. (1988), 'Multiple Victimisation' in M. Maguire and J. Pointing (eds), *Victims of Crime: A New Deal?,* Open University Press, Milton Keynes.

Giddens, A. (1990), *The Consequences of Modernity*, Polity Press, Cambridge.

Giddens, A. (1991), *Modernity and Self-Identity,* Basil Blackwell, Oxford.

Giddens, A. (1998), *The Third Way*, Polity, Oxford.

GMC County Structure Plan, 1975.

Gold, J.R. (1982), 'Territoriality and Human Spatial Behaviour', *Progress in Human Geography*, vol. 6, no. i.

Greenwood, W. (1987), *Love on the Dole*, Penguin Books Ltd, Middlesex.

Gregory, D. (1994), *Geographical Imagination*, Blackwell, Cambridge, MA.

HMSO (1998), *Crime and Disorder Act 1998*, HMSO Publications.

Hampson, C.P. (1930), *Salford Through the Ages. The Fons et Origio of an Industrial City*, E.J.Morten, Manchester.

Hills, J. (1995), *Inquiry into Income and Wealth - Volume Two. A Summary of the Evidence*, Joseph Rowntree Foundation.

Hills, J. (1998), *Income and Wealth: The Latest Evidence*, Joseph Rowntree Foundation.

Hirschfield, A. (1994), 'Crime and the Spatial Concentration of Disadvantage in Northern Britain: An Analysis Using G.I.S.' *Urban Research and Policy Evaluation Regional Laboratory Working Paper 44*, University of Liverpool, Liverpool.

Hirschfield, A. (1994), 'Using the 1991 Population Census to Study Deprivation' in *Planning Practice and Research*, vol. 9, no. 1.

Hobbs, D. (1989), *Doing the Business*, Oxford University Press, Oxford.

Hoggett, P. (ed) (1997), *Contested Communities*, Policy Press, Bristol.

Hope, T. (1994), 'Communities, Crime and Inequality in England and Wales', paper presented to the 22nd Annual Cropwood Round-table Conference *Preventing Crime and Disorder*.

Hope, T. (1995), 'Community Crime Prevention' in M. Tonry and D.P. Farrington *Building a Safer Society - Strategic Approaches to Crime Prevention: Crime and Justice*, vol 19, University of Chicago, Chicago.

Hope, T. and Shaw, M. (eds) (1988), *Communities and Crime Reduction*, HMSO, London.

Hope, T. and Hough, M. (1988), 'Area, Crime, and Incivility: A Profile From The British Crime Survey', in T. Hope and M. Shaw, (eds), *Communities and Crime Reduction*, HMSO, London.

Hollway, W. and Jefferson, T. (1997), 'The Risk Society in an Age of Anxiety: Situating the Fear of Crime', *British Journal of Sociology*, vol. 48, no. 2, June.

Home Office (1993), *A Practical Guide to Crime Prevention for Local Partnerships*.

Hutton, W. (1995), *The State We're In*, Jonathon Cape, London.

Karmen, A. (1990), *Crime Victims: An Introduction to Victimology*, Brooks Cole, Pacific Grove, Calif.

Independent on Sunday (1994), 'Fear Rules in No Go Britain', April 17th.

Institute of Social Research, University of Salford (1994, *Crime in Salford 2: Community Safety and the Protection of Residential and Commercial Property in Salford in 1994*, report to the City of Salford.

LGMB/LGA (1997) *Crime - The Local Solution, Current Practice,* March, London: Local Government Association and Local Government Management Board for Crime,

Lash, S. and Urry, J. (1994), *Economies of Signs and Space*, Sage, London.

Lee, J. (1981), 'Some Structural Aspects of Police Deviance in Relation to Minority Groups' in C. Shearing (ed.), *Organisational Police Deviance*, Toronto, Butterworth.

Lewis, D. and Salem, G. (1986), *Fear of Crime: Incivility and the Production of a Social Problem*, Transaction Books, New Brunswick, N.J.

Luhmann, N. (1989), 'Familiarity, Confidence, Trust: Problems and Alternatives' in D. Gambetta (ed), *Trust: Making and Breaking Co-operative Relations,* Basil Blackwell, London.

Malpass, P and Means, R (eds) (1993), *Implementing Housing Policy.*

Manchester and Salford Inner City Partnership Research Group (1978), *Manchester and Salford Inner Area Study.*

Manchester TEC (1995), *Labour Market Assessment Summary 1994-5.*

Massey, D. (1994*) Space, Place and Gender.* Polity Press: Cambridge.

Matthews, R. (1992), 'Replacing Broken Windows: Crime, Incivilities and Urban Change', in R. Matthews and J. Young (eds), *Issues in Realist Criminology,* Sage, London.

Mawby, R. and Walklate, S. (1994), *Critical Victimology*, Sage, London.

Maynard, W. (1994), *Witness Intimidation: Strategies for Prevention*, Police Research Group Crime Detection Series Paper 55, HMSO, London.

McGrady, S. (1994), *Difficult-to-let Housing Association Properties in Higher Broughton and Salford,* submitted to the Housing Management Specialist Unit D.A.S.H. Course, University College Salford.

Merry, S. (1981), *Urban Danger*, Temple University Press, Philadelphia.

Middleton (1991), *Cities in Transition.*

Misztal, B. (1996), *Trust in Modern Societies,* Polity, Oxford.

Monaghan, L., Taylor, I. and Walklate, S. (1994), *Crime Audit Salford 1994* report to Salford City Council.

Murray, C. (1990), *The Emerging British Underclass*, IEA, London.

National Board for Crime Prevention (1994), *Wise after the Event: Tackling Repeat Victimisation.*

Nelken, D. (1994), 'Women Can You Trust? The Future of Comparative Criminology', in D. Nelken (ed.), *The Futures of Criminology*, Sage, London.

Newburn, T. (1993), *The Long-Term Needs of Victims: A Review of the Literature*, Home Office RPU Paper 80.

Pollard, C. (1997), Zero Tolerance: Short Term Fix, Long Term Liability? in N. Dennis (ed.), *Zero Tolerance: Policing a Free Society*, IEA, London.

Reisman, L. (1964), *The Urban Process - Cities in Industrial Societies*, Collier Macmillan.

Roberts, R. (1973), *The Classic Slum,* Penguin, Harmondsworth.

Salford Community Health Project (1994), *10 Year Report,* Salford Centre for Health Promotion.

Salford Health Authority (undated), *Action for Better Health Salford Health Authorities' Purchasing Plan 1993/94.*

Salford Health Authority (undated), *Salford and Trafford Health Authorities' Purchasing Plans Overview 1994/95.*

Salford Quays Heritage Centre (1994), *Barbary Coast Re-visited: A Book by Ordsall about Ordsall - The Heart of Salford Docklands.*

Salford Quays Heritage Centre (1992), *Bridging the Years: A History of Trafford Park and Salford Docks by Those Who Lived and Worked in the Area,* Manchester Free Press, Manchester.

Sampson, A. et al. (1988), 'Crime, Localities and the Multi-Agency Approach'. *British Journal of Criminology*, vol. 28, no. 4, pp. 478-493.

Satwiko,L.W. (1992), *Inner City Policy and the Enterprise Zone: The Case of Salford EZ,* PhD Thesis, Dept of Geography, May.

Savage, M. et al. (1987), 'Locality Research; The Sussex Programme on Economic Restructuring, Social Change and the Locality', *The Quarterly Journal of Social Affairs*, vol. 3, no. 1, pp. 27-51.

Sennett, R. (1990), *The Conscience of the Eye: The Design and Social Life of Cities*, Faber and Faber, London.

Sennett, R. (1998), *The Corrosion of Character*, W.W. Norton, New York.

Shapland, J., and Vagg, J. (1988), *Policing by the Public*, Routledge, London.

Skogan, W.G. (1988), 'Community Organisations and Crime' in M. Tonry and N. Morris (eds), *Crime and Justice: A Review of Research*, University of Chicago Press, Chicago.

Social Exclusion Unit (1998), *Bringing Britain Together*, HMSO, London.

Stanko, E.A. (1997), 'Safety Talk: Conceptualising Women's Risk Assessment as a "Technology of the Soul"', *Theoretical Criminology,* vol. 1, no. 4, pp. 479-99.

Taylor, I. R. (1996), 'Fear of Crime, Urban Fortunes and Suburban Social Movements: Some Reflections from Manchester', *Sociology*, vol.30, no. 2. pp. 317-37.

Taylor, I.R. (1997), 'Crime, Anxiety, and Locality: Responding to the Condition of England at the End of the Century', *Theoretical Criminology*, vol. 1, no. 1, pp. 53-76.

Taylor, I.R., Evans, K. and Fraser, P. (1996), *A Tale of Two Cities*, Routledge, London.

Tomlinson, V.I. (1973), *Salford in Pictures*, E.J. Morten, Manchester.

Tonry, M. and Morris, N. (eds), *Crime and Justice: A Review of Research*, University of Chicago Press, Chicago.

Tonry, M. and Farrington, D.P. (1995), 'Building a Safer Society - Strategic Approaches to Crime Prevention', *Crime and Justice*, vol. 19, University of Chicago, Chicago.

Townsend, P. (1992), *The Black Report: Inequalities in Health*, London, Penguin.

Trickett, A. et al. (1992), 'What is Different About High Crime Areas', *British Journal of Criminology*, Winter.

Wachs, E. (1988), *Crime-Victim Stories: New York City's Urban Folklore*, Indiana University Press, Bloomington.

Walklate, S. (1990), 'Researching Victims of Crime: Critical Victimiology', *Social Justice*, vol. 17, no. 3.

Walklate, S. (1997), 'Crime and Community: Fear or Trust?', plenary presentation to the Australia and New Zealand Annual Criminology Conference, July, Brisbane.

Walklate, S. (1998), 'Excavating the Fear of Crime: Fear, Anxiety or Trust?', *Theoretical Criminology*, vol. 2, no. 4, November.

Ward, C. (1985), *When We Build Again: Let's Have Housing That Works!*, Pluto, London.

Williams, R. (1977), *Marxism and Literature*, Oxford University Press, Oxford.

Working Class Movement Library (undated), *Chartism in Salford*, Salford City Council, Cultural Services Department.

Author Index